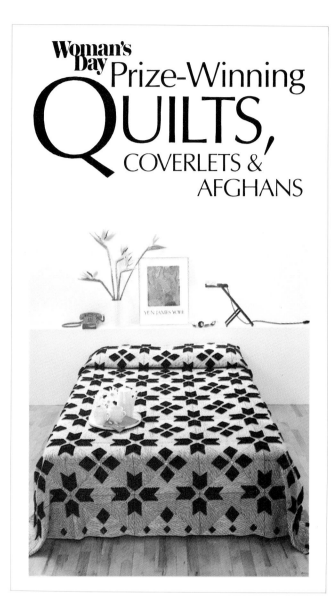

Woman's Day
Prize-Winning
QUILTS,
COVERLETS &
AFGHANS

![Woman's Day] Prize-Winning

QUILTS,
COVERLETS &
AFGHANS

edited by Julie Houston

SEDGEWOOD PRESS

NEW YORK

For CBS Inc.

Editorial Director: *Dina von Zweck*

Editor: *Julie Houston*

Project Coordinator: *Lisa LeFever*

How-to-Writer: *Ellen Liberles*

Illustrator: *Patrick J. O'Brien*

For Sedgewood Press

Editorial Director, Sedgewood Press: *Jane Ross*

Project Director: *Virginia Colton*

Supervising Editor: *Gale Kremer*

Designer: *Bentwood Studio/Jos. Trautwein*

Production Manager: *Bill Rose*

Photography

Robert H. Epstein, Inc. 27, 33, 47, 67, 75, 91, 135, 195, 213, 217, 231.

Woman's Day Studio. All other photographs.

Distributed in the Trade by Van Nostrand Reinhold.
ISBN 0-442-28091-2
Library of Congress Catalog Number 81-71012.
Manufactured in the United States of America.

Contents

Editor's Introduction

From Tennessee to Illinois, from Massachusetts to California, when the entries for the *Woman's Day* Afghan and Coverlet contest began pouring in, it was instantly apparent that this would be one of the most exciting collections of needlework ever assembled, a moving and inspiring glimpse into the spirit of inventive Americans, their energy and ingenuity flowing through every stitch of every design.

That a book should emerge from so unique a creative harvest is cause for celebration. It adds a fresh, new dimension to the picture we have of a very traditional, and very popular, area of needlework, but it also reveals something deeper, well below the surface eventfulness of a contest, about the creative process as it was experienced by each winner —indeed, by each contestant. Nothing quite equals a book for gaining such insight. In the course of selecting and assembling the thirty-five projects included here—all prize-winners and representative in every way of the remarkable scope and diversity of *all* the entries submitted— we were able to go back to the designers themselves for a first-hand description of how each piece came about, of hidden details that show, in the finished work, only as a design executed to perfection.

Apart from the individuality of the designs there is diversity in other key areas as well.

First, there is the variety of actual terms used to describe a finished piece—lap throw, bedspread, comforter, bridal quilt, baby quilt, to name a few—all clearly reflecting the freedom that this category of needlework offers for personal interpretation.

Sewing skills are also diverse, as are the roads travelled to acquire them. Whether straight sewing, embroidery, knitting, crochet or a combination, the techniques used by the contestants are at some times simple, at others complex, depending entirely on the inclination or interests of the designer. Where one person will stay with a single stitch throughout, another will use hundreds to create a design, both with equally handsome results. Sometimes techniques are treated primarily as "tools"—as the means to an end—an approach exemplified by Rhue Luna's appliquéd *Landscape Scenes* on page 88 and Gloria Morris' knitted *Taos Sunrise* on page 212. Techniques in some works appear to be an end in themselves, so integral are they to the overall effect. For dramatic examples see Sarah Morgret's *Embroidered Crazy Quilt* on page 115 and Bernice Hampson's *Sampler in Pastels* on page 202.

Interestingly, it did not seem to matter whether a designer had "inherited" her skills from family members, shared the learning process with friends, or simply picked them up on her own (or *his* own, as did John Meren, whose story is told on page 126). What *did* seem to matter was that each person had the courage, confidence and perseverance to rip

out, experiment, improvise, and even start over if necessary, to achieve the best results possible with their own original designs.

Contributing significantly to the diversity of this marvelous collection were the many different origins of the designs—where they came from and how they were inspired. Many are emphatically regional—for example, Pamela Joseph's appliquéd *Alaskan Baby Quilt* on page 72, Janet Schields' pieced *Bear Paw Quilt* from Pike County in Pennsylvania, which appears on page 17, and Barbara Boulton's knitted *Sea and Shells* afghan, on page 229, from Sanibel Island, off the coast of Florida. The impulse for others was aroused in a more general way by the colors and shapes found in nature through the seasons, impressions aptly captured in Grace Stinton's appliquéd *Autumn Harvest* on page 66 and Sylvia Mater's crocheted *Flower Fantasy* on page 160. Some designers chose home decorating as their springboard, deliberately selecting colors and patterns to coordinate with furniture and decor. Eligene Buchanan matched her *Granny Variation* afghan (page 144) with the fabric pattern of an upholstered chair; Arleta Freeman designed her *Cotton and Satin Laced Quilt* (page 44) to complement a new bedroom suite. Then there are the heartwarming designs that commemorate sentimental occasions or fond memories—Jane Soulant planning her *Twisted Ribbons* bridal quilt (page 83) for her daughter's wedding; Beatrice Thompson recalling moments from her past in her crocheted *Pictorial Memories* (page 178).

In the incredible expanse of territory covered in search of design sources, there should be new incentive for anyone interested in pursuing patterns of her own.

Finally, and among the most important explanations for diversity, there is the human factor, the individual designers who make this such an extraordinary cross-section of contemporary sewing and needlework. Collectively, the stories they have shared about themselves and their work reveals a conscientious group of people, working hard to raise families, support themselves and keep things going from day to day and year to year. Accustomed to giving of themselves generously and spontaneously, they put the same spirit into their creative endeavors, reveling in the tradition—and the challenge—of work that is exquisitely done, beautiful to see and, wonder among wonders, ultimately practical.

As these thirty-five pieces so triumphantly testify, the art of making quilts, coverlets and afghans is alive, and thriving. Far from imitative, today's designers are strikingly imaginative, independent and free-thinking, continuing to tap the best of needlework's rich past while generating a vitality of design firmly rooted in the present.

JULIE HOUSTON
Project Editor

PART I Sewn & Embroidered Designs

For a general guide to techniques involved in making these quilts, see pages 234-242.

MARINER'S COMPASS

A lap throw by Janet S. Manahan of Sutton, Massachusetts

This innovative treatment of the traditional Mariner's Compass motif combines bright calico prints in four bold repeats with an intricate, deep-bordered quilting design.

about
Janet S. Manahan

Janet Manahan offers an interesting explanation for her special ability to render such an exquisite interpretation of a perennial favorite among quilting designs. Because she is a self-taught quilter, as were many pioneer women of long ago, she counts on her imagination to overcome the "pitfalls" that quilting frequently presents. When they arise, she says, she shifts her approach and "transposes herself in time to try to solve the problems with the tools and knowledge probably available to the average eighteenth century farm woman." The skillfully executed result confirms her success with this highly original way of thinking.

SIZE Lap quilt (4 blocks) as shown, about 53″ square; full-sized quilt (12 blocks), about 73″ x 93″.

MATERIALS One ½″-thick 66″ x 96″ polyester quilt batt for lap quilt or one 81″ x 96″ batt for full-sized quilt; 4½ [9] yds. (yardage for full-sized quilt is in brackets) 45″-wide unbleached muslin for background, lining, binding and some appliqué; 45″-wide small-print cotton or cotton-blend fabrics for appliqué and borders (referring to Applique Diagram: ½ [1] yd. color A, B is included in border print yardage, C is included in corner print yardage, ⅜ [⅞] yd. D, E is included in muslin yardage, ¼ [⅜] yd. F, 1 [2] yd. border print, ½ [1⅛] yd. corner print; matching sewing threads; white quilting thread; thin cardboard for patterns; dressmaker's carbon paper and tracing wheel; tracing paper; quilting frame (available at Sears or craft stores).

APPLIQUÉD BLOCKS For each block, cut a 21″ square from muslin for background. Enlarge patterns (see How to Enlarge Patterns, page 255) and cut from cardboard. Trace around cardboard patterns on right side of fabric, leaving at least ½″ between pieces as follows: following Appliqué

NOTE *Quilt is composed of four blocks for lap size or twelve blocks for full size, print borders and corner squares. Each block is appliquéd separately, then blocks are joined and borders and corner squares are added. Top, batt and lining are basted together and quilted; edges are then bound.*

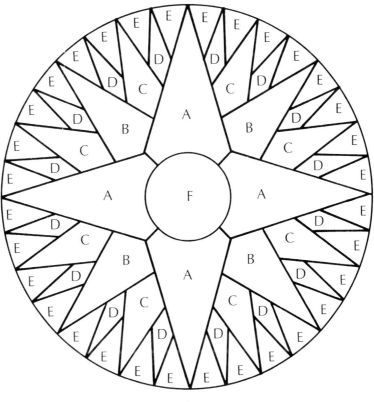

APPLIQUÉ DIAGRAM

Diagram, cut 4 color A pieces, 4 B pieces, 8 C, 16 D and 16 E, adding ¼″ seam allowance all around. Also cut 5″-diameter circle pattern (seam allowance included). Cut one F circle. Turn under and press seam allowance of F, clipping seam allowance. Turn under and press edges on other pieces as follows: long side edges and short edge X on A pieces, long side edges on B, C and D pieces, short edges only on E pieces. Assemble and pin pieces, as shown on Appliqué Diagram, onto center of muslin background, lapping pressed edges over raw edges and butting edges X. Appliqué pieces with tiny stitches. Make 4 [12] blocks in all.

Each square = 1″ square

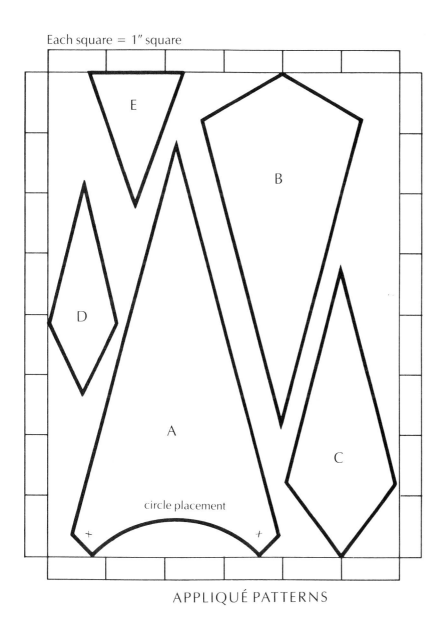

APPLIQUÉ PATTERNS

TO ASSEMBLE BLOCKS With right sides facing, stitch two blocks together with ½″ seams along one edge. For lap quilt, stitch together other two blocks; then, matching center corners carefully, stitch together to form square. For full quilt, join blocks into four strips of three blocks each; then join strips to form top three blocks wide by four blocks long, carefully matching corners as you join.

QUILTING PATTERNS Enlarge Quilting Patterns on tracing paper. With light-colored carbon paper and tracing wheel, transfer a corner pattern to each corner of each block.

NOTE *For full quilt it may be necessary to piece borders.*
Borders *From color B, cut two 7″-wide strips the length of assembled top and two 7″-wide strips the width of top. From C, cut four 7″-square corner pieces. With ½″ seams, attach top and bottom borders; corner square to each end of side borders; side borders to quilt, matching seams at corners.*

Each square = 1″ square

QUILTING PATTERNS

Transfer border patterns to borders, placing flower in each corner and extending interlocking pattern to length of borders, adjusting pattern at center of each border to fit, if necessary.

TO ASSEMBLE QUILT Cut and piece muslin lining to same size as top. Cut quilt batt to about 2″ larger all around than lining. Assemble top, batt and lining, with batt centered in middle and top panel centered on batt and lining. Baste layers together from top corners diagonally across to opposite lower corners, then across center from edge to edge in both directions.

TO QUILT Following directions that come with frame, mount quilt on frame. Working from center out, quilt tiny running stitches through all layers. Quilt ⅛″ in from all edges of each appliquéd piece, then quilt ⅛″ outside outer edge of mariner's compass. Quilt all marked designs and ¼″ inside inner edge of color B borders.

FINISHING Trim batt to same size as lining. From muslin, cut and piece two 2″-wide strips for binding to fit two side edges of quilt. With right sides together, making ½″ seams, stitch binding to quilt side edges, then, leaving ½″ binding showing on right side, fold in half to wrong side, turn in ½″ seam allowance and stitch hem. Cut and piece two strips 1″ longer than top and bottom edges. Turn in ends ½″ and bind remaining quilt edges. Remove all basting threads.

BEAR PAW QUILT

A bedspread by Janet F. Schields of Milford, Pennsylvania

Pieced repeats of the traditional "bear paw" motif alternate with fifteen quilted wildlife "sketches" to create a rustic, earth-tone design. Quilted bear tracks continue around the border.

about Janet F. Schields

Janet Schields' move from the suburbs of Long Island to rural Pennsylvania brought her closer than ever to the joys of outdoor life; it also provides a wealth of inspiration for her needlework designs. In planning her design, she "decided to incorporate an interest in the flowers and fauna of Pike County," and simply began sketching scenes from memory and experience, observing nature at first hand. A self-taught quilter, she kept the sketches as simple as possible for easy adaptation to quilting, and worked square-by-square in a "quilt as you go" procedure.

SIZE About 80 x 94″.

MATERIALS One ½″-thick 90 x 108″ polyester quilt batt; 4½ yds. 45″-wide unbleached muslin for plain quilted blocks and pieced blocks; 45″-wide cotton or cotton-blend print fabrics: ¾ yd. each brown and green prints for pieced blocks, 7½ yds. tan print for pieced blocks, border and lining; white and brown sewing threads; iron-on transfer pencil if desired; dressmaker's carbon paper and tracing wheel.

PIECED BLOCKS: Cutting Cutting brown print from selvage to selvage, cut four 2¼″-wide strips, twenty 4½″ squares and five 2¼″ squares. Keeping colors separate, repeat with green and tan prints. From muslin, cut twelve 2¼″-wide strips from selvage to selvage, sixty 2½″ squares and sixty 2½″ x 6½″ rectangles.

Piecing Make ¼″ seams throughout. Stitching strips lengthwise, stitch together 4 muslin strips and 4 brown print strips, alternating them. Carefully trim away ¼″ seam allowance across top and bottom (45″-long) edges, so that all strips are 1¾″ wide. Following dimensions on Diagram for Two-color Squares, using ruler and pencil, carefully mark top edge of joined strips into one 1¾″ section, twelve 3½″ sections and one 1¾″ section. Repeat along bottom edge, then mark diagonal lines as shown. Cut along markings. You will be using 80 of the resulting eighty-eight 2½″ squares. In the same manner, make 2-color squares of muslin with green and with tan prints.

NOTE *Quilt is composed of thirty 14″ square blocks: 15 blocks pieced in muslin and print in bear paw pattern and 15 blocks quilted in a woodland scene on muslin (see NOTE at Quilted Plain Blocks, page 21). A quilting frame is unnecessary because each block is worked separately: pieced, assembled with batt and lining, then quilted. Completed blocks are stitched together and raw edges of lining on each block are finished by hand. Border is assembled, quilted and stitched in place.*

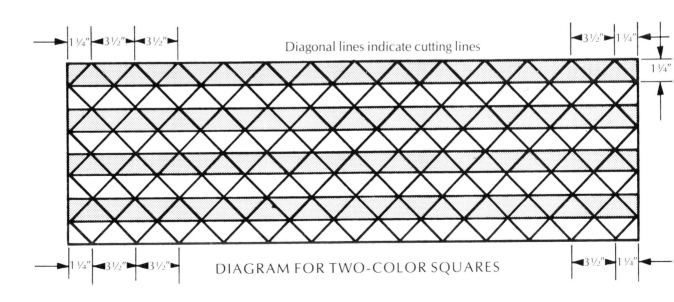

DIAGRAM FOR TWO-COLOR SQUARES

ASSEMBLY DIAGRAMS

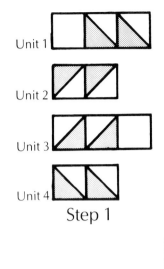

Step 1

Following steps of assembly diagrams, stitch two 2-color squares and a muslin square together for unit 1. Make another unit 1. Make two each of units 2, 3 and 4. For step 2, stitch a unit 1 and unit 2 together as shown. For step 3, add a brown print 4½" square. For step 4, add muslin rectangle. Add pieces as shown in steps 5, 6 and 7 to complete section A. For step 8, stitch 2 muslin rectangles to a brown print 2½" square for center section. Work steps 1 through 7 again for section B. Stitch edges X on sections A and B to each side of center section (step 8) to complete block. Make 4 more blocks with brown print, 5 blocks each with green and tan prints.

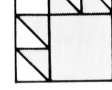

Step 2

Step 3

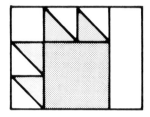

Step 4

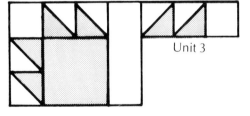

Step 5

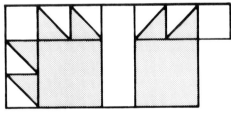

Step 6

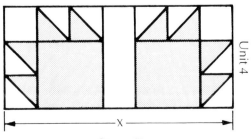

Step 7
(Section A or B)

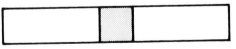

Step 8
(Center Section)

Assembling and Quilting Cut 15″ square each from tan print and from batt. Stack tan print lining (wrong side up), batt and pieced top (right side up). Baste together from top corners diagonally across to opposite lower corners, then across center from edge to opposite edge in both directions.

Using brown thread, quilt block by working small running stitches through all layers, following broken lines on Quilting Block Diagram.

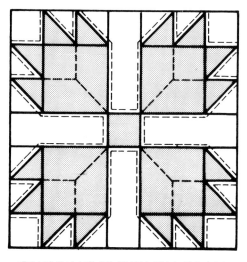

QUILTING BLOCK DIAGRAM

QUILTED PLAIN BLOCKS For each block, cut a 15″ square each from muslin, batt and tan print. Enlarge design pattern (see How to Enlarge Patterns, p. 255). With dress-maker's carbon and stylus such as empty cartridge from ballpoint pen, trace design onto muslin; or trace design onto tracing paper with an iron-on transfer pencil, reverse design and iron just long enough so that you mark the muslin without scorching it.

Stack muslin, batt and lining and baste together as for pieced block.

Quilting Using brown thread, quilt entire design, following lines with tiny running stitches. For dots, such as eyes on bear, work French knots.

Make 15 quilted blocks.

NOTE *On original quilt, a different woodland scene was used for each of the 15 blocks. Because of space limitations and the difficulty for readers to enlarge so many designs, one scene, a bear, has been selected to use for all 15 quilted blocks. If you prefer different scenes, you can draw or trace your own 14″-square scenes, following the photograph as a guide. (Travel, nature and sport-hunting magazines may be other good sources for woodland scenes to copy.)*

Each square – 1" square

QUILTING DESIGN

TO ASSEMBLE QUILT TOP Trim batt on each block ¼″ smaller on each side than lining and top. Arrange blocks, alternating pieced and quilted blocks to form top panel 5 blocks by 6 blocks (see photograph). Hold 2 blocks together with right sides facing; making ¼″ seam, stitch 2 adjacent edges, stitching through top squares only (lining will be finished by hand and batts will butt when blocks are opened out). Continue to stitch blocks together to form vertical or horizontal strips, then stitch strips together to form quilt top,

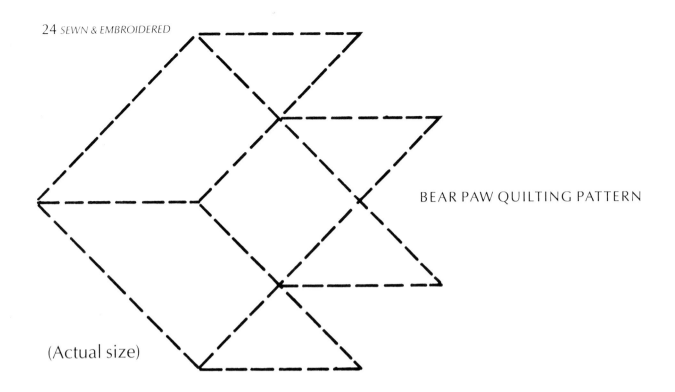

BEAR PAW QUILTING PATTERN

(Actual size)

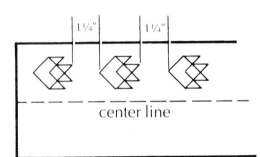

BORDER DIAGRAM

carefully matching corners of blocks. To finish edges of lining squares, turn under one seam allowance and lap it over seam allowance on adjacent edge; stitch hem. Finish all raw edges in this manner except those on outer edges of quilt.

BORDER Cut 2 batt strips 5″ wide by length of quilt. Cut 2 tan print strips 11″ wide by length of quilt.

Using basting threads or pins, mark lengthwise center line on a fabric strip. Using dressmaker's carbon and tracing wheel, transfer bear paw quilting pattern 14 times, centered and evenly spaced about 1¼″ apart, along half the width of strips (see Border Diagram). Fold fabric strip in half over a batt strip (long edges of fabric will extend ½″ beyond long edges of batt for seam allowance). Baste layers together. Quilt bear paws. Repeat with other strip and batt. With right sides together, stitch a border to each side of quilt top, stitching through top layers only. Fold border out, turn in raw edge on wrong side and stitch hem.

Cut two 5″-wide batt strips the width of quilt (include side borders). Cut 2 tan print strips 11″ wide and 1″ longer than width of quilt. Mark fabric strips with 13 bear paws each and quilt as before. Stitch borders to ends of quilt, finish edges on wrong side, then turn in seam allowance at ends and stitch hem. Remove all basting threads.

TRIPLE IRISH CHAIN COVERLET

A pieced quilt by Jane Bishop Wright of Twin Falls, Idaho

An unusual quilting pattern not only emphasizes stunning piecework — it makes such an interesting design that the quilt becomes reversible.

about
Jane Bishop Wright

Jane Bishop Wright's grandmother was more than her inspiration; she was also her sole motivation for making this prize quilt. In 1974, a year before Jane's high school graduation, her grandmother could not see well enough to piece a quilt, something she had lovingly done for each of her grandchildren to mark that occasion. To ease her disappointment, Jane agreed to make the quilt herself, if they could pick out the fabrics together, all from scraps saved over the years — from grandmother's apron, mother's favorite dress, Jane's first kindergarten outfit, fabric from her bridemaids' dresses. "Triple Irish chain" is her grandmother's original design; Jane developed her own way of setting it together and her own quilting pattern.

NOTE *Quilt is composed of 30 piecework blocks, fifteen each of 2 different designs. Each block is pieced separately, then joined, alternating designs, to form center panel 5 blocks wide by 6 blocks long; then border strips are added. Top, batt and lining are basted together and quilted.*

SIZE About 85″ x 100″, finished. Each block measures about 14⅝″ square.

MATERIALS One ½″-thick 90″ x 108″ polyester quilt batt; king-size sheet in pale purple or other coordinating color for lining; 45″-wide cotton-blend fabric: 2 yds. dark shade of purple (or other main color), 1¾ yds. light shade of purple (or other main color), ⅝ yd. medium shade of purple (or other main color), 3½ yds. white; small scraps of prints in many different colors and patterns; quilting thread; matching sewing thread; ruler; quilting frame (available at Sears and craft stores).

BLOCK 1 (Small Squares) **Cutting** selvage to selvage, cut 2⅛″-wide strips of white and of dark and medium purple. Cutting off as needed, cut strips into 2⅛″ squares, having 37 white squares, 12 dark purple squares and 4 medium purple squares for each Block 1. Also cut twenty-eight 2⅛″ squares from assorted prints for each block.

ASSEMBLY DIAGRAM FOR
BLOCK 1 (SMALL SQUARES)

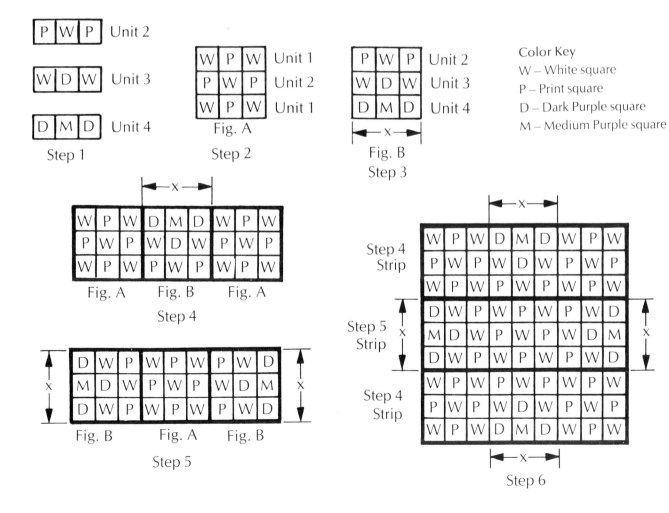

Color Key
W – White square
P – Print square
D – Dark Purple square
M – Medium Purple square

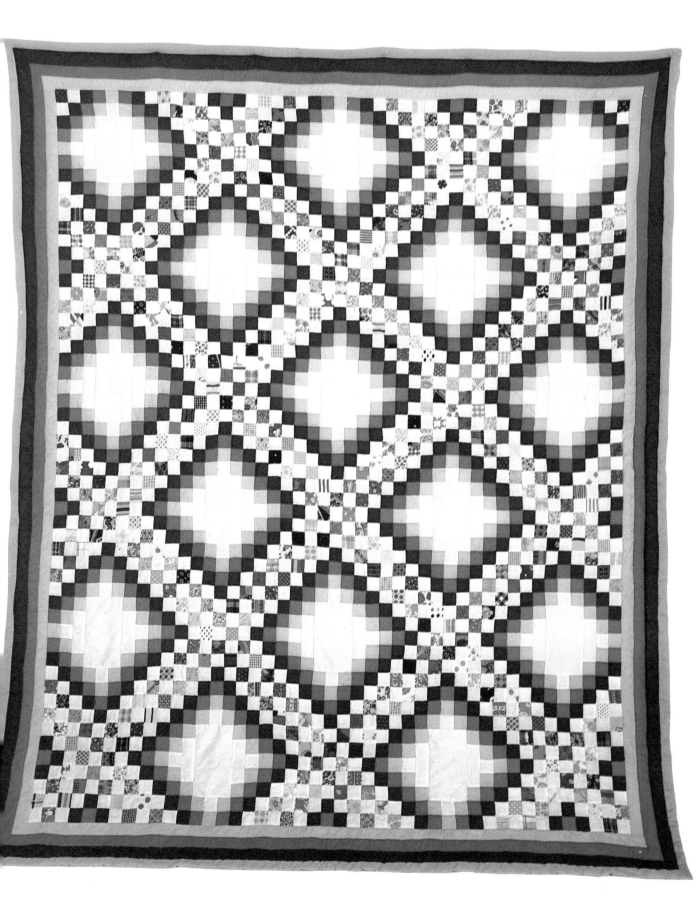

Piecing Make ¼″ seams throughout. Match corners carefully. Following steps of assembly diagrams, stitch 1 print and 2 white squares together for unit 1. Make 9 more units 1. Make 9 units 2; make 4 each of units 3 and 4. For step 2, stitch together a unit 1, a unit 2 and another unit 1 (figure A formed). Make 4 more figures A. For step 3, stitch together a unit 2, a unit 3 and a unit 4 (figure B; note position of side X). Make 3 more figures B. For step 4, stitch together a figure A, figure B (upside-down; note side X) and another figure A. Make another strip in same manner. For step 5, stitch together figure B (note side X), figure A, another figure B (note side X). For step 6, stitch together a step 4 strip, a step 5 strip and another step 4 strip (note side X) to complete block.

Make 14 more blocks in same manner.

BLOCK 2 (Squares and Rectangles): **Cutting** From white, cut a rectangle 5⅜″ x 8⅝″ for each block. Cutting from selvage to selvage, cut 2⅛″-wide strips of white, and dark, medium and light shades of purple. From white strip, cut 2 rectangles 2⅛″ x 5⅜″ for each block. Cutting off as needed, cut remaining strips into 2⅛″ squares, having 12 white, 12 dark purple, 16 medium purple and 16 light purple squares for each block. Cut four 2⅛″ squares from assorted prints for each block.

Piecing Make ¼″ seams throughout. Match corners carefully. Following steps of assembly diagrams, make 2 each of units 1, 2, 3 (using small white rectangle at center) and 4. For step 2, stitch together a unit 1, unit 2 and unit 3 (figure A; note side Y). Make another figure A. For step 3, stitch

ASSEMBLY DIAGRAM FOR
BLOCK 2 (WITH RECTANGLES)

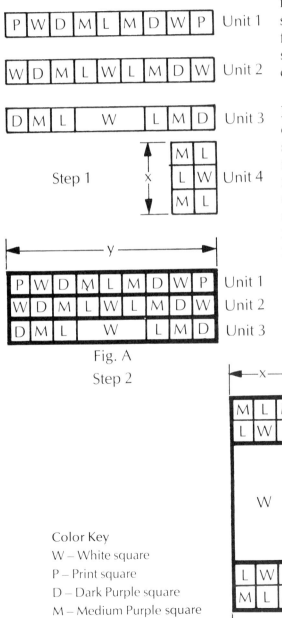

Color Key
W – White square
P – Print square
D – Dark Purple square
M – Medium Purple square
L – Light Purple square

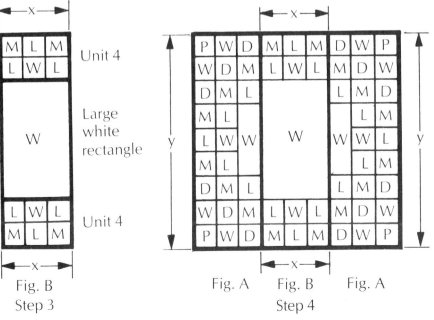

Fig. B
Step 3

Fig. A   Fig. B   Fig. A
Step 4

together a unit 4 (note side X), large white rectangle and another unit 4 (note side X) to form figure B. For step 4, stitch together figures A, B and A, noting sides X and Y.

Make 14 more blocks in same manner.

TO ASSEMBLE TOP Following Placement Diagram, stitch blocks together with ¼″ seams, carefully matching seams and corners, to form top 5 blocks wide by 6 blocks long.

BLOCKS From light purple, cut four 2⅛″-wide border strips, two of them 3½″ longer than width and two 3½″ longer than length of quilt top, piecing as necessary for length. With right sides together, making ¼″ seams, center and stitch strips to quilt top edges, mitering corners. Trim away excess fabric at corners.

From medium purple, cut a 2⅛″-wide border strip for each edge, each 3½″ longer than last strip joined. Stitch strips in place as before, mitering corners.

From dark purple, cut a 2⅛″-wide border strip for each edge, each 3½″ longer than last strip joined. Stitch strips in place as before.

TO ASSEMBLE QUILT Cut sheet to make lining 89″ x 104″. Cut quilt batt same size as lining. Assemble top, batt and lining with batt centered in the middle and top centered on batt and lining. Baste layers together from top corners diagonally across to opposite lower corners, then across center from edge to edge in both directions.

TO QUILT Following directions that come with frame, mount quilt on frame. Working from quilt center outward, quilt tiny running stitches through all layers as follows: On Block 1, quilt two diagonal lines across entire block from lower left corner to upper right corner, stitching through diagonal center of each print square; extend lines onto corner print squares of each surrounding Block 2. Quilt two diagonal lines across block from lower right corner to upper left corner, stitching diagonally across print squares as before.

On Block 2, quilt around each pieced section along seamline, except for corner print square, and also work around medium and dark purple squares at center of each edge of Block 1. On borders, quilt along each seamline between border strips.

FINISHING Trim quilt batt to 85″ x 100″. Fold excess lining fabric to right side of quilt over quilt batt and top edges. Leaving 1½″ border showing all around, turn under raw edges and stitch in place, mitering the corners. Remove all basting threads.

1	2	1	2	1
2	1	2	1	2
1	2	1	2	1
2	1	2	1	2
1	2	1	2	1
2	1	2	1	2

PLACEMENT
DIAGRAM

TRADITIONAL QUILT BLOCKS

A pieced and quilted coverlet by Lila Rostenberg of Little Rock, Arkansas

Thirty-two design blocks surround a central, focal block in this, the very first quilt made by its designer.

about
Lila Rostenberg

Lila Rostenberg's beautiful quilt proudly fulfills her goal "to use traditional blocks but to arrange and interrelate them for a new look." The result is a strikingly fresh and contemporary interpretation of several popular quilt motifs, "hand-pieced and hand-quilted," she explains, "because those are the techniques I wanted to learn at the time." Using a book of traditional patterns for reference, Lila planned her design on graph paper and chose fabrics to match her color scheme. "This quilt has led to many exciting things for me. From it, I have gone on to making and selling many quilts and designs. I have made many new friends through teaching, workshops and our newly-formed Arkansas Quilter's Guild (of which I was the first president)."

SIZE About 67″ x 67″, finished.

MATERIALS One ½″-thick 81″ x 96″ polyester quilt batt; 45″-wide cotton or cotton-blend fabric: 5 yds. yellow print (YP) for lining and some pieces, 2½ yds. each of red print (RP) for border sections and some pieces and bright blue (B) for binding and some pieces, 1 yd. each of yellow (Y), black print (BP) and bright gold print (GP), ¼ yd. each of maroon (M) and red (R); matching sewing threads; yellow quilting thread; quilting frame (available at Sears or craft stores); dressmaker's carbon paper and tracing wheel; thin cardboard; brown wrapping paper; yardstick or ruler.

CENTER BLOCK Enlarge pattern on page 35 (see How to Enlarge Patterns, page 255). Cut from cardboard. Trace around cardboard pattern on right side of fabrics, leaving at least ½″ between pieces, tracing 4 diamond pieces each on RP and YP. Cut out, adding ¼″ seam allowance all around; mark sides **a** (inner edges that are joined to form unit 1) with pins or chalk. From B cut an 11″ square (includes ¼″ seam allowance all around) and 4 strips 1″ x 16½″. Cut two 6½″ squares each from Y and BP; cut each square in half diagonally to form two triangles.

Following assembly diagram and making ¼″ seams, stitch together **a** sides of diamond pieces, alternating colors, to form unit 1. Take care to match points carefully. For unit 2,

NOTE *Quilt is composed of a 16″-square pieced center block and thirty-two 8″-square pieced design blocks. Each block is pieced separately, then joined to form center panel; quilt top square is completed with 8″ shaped strips of background fabric and 8 half blocks. Top, batt and lining are assembled and quilted. Edges are bound with narrow border.*

ASSEMBLY OF
CENTER BLOCK

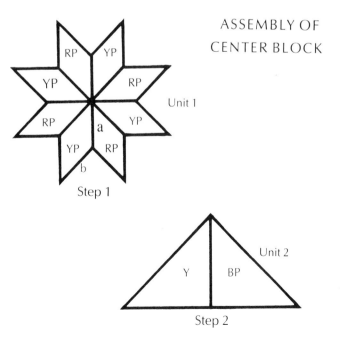

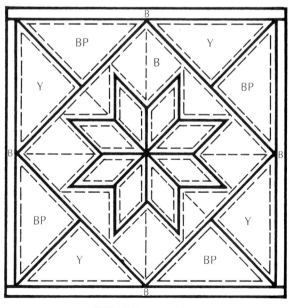

CENTER BLOCK

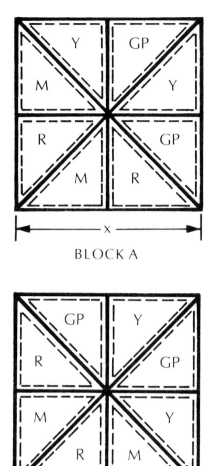

BLOCK A

BLOCK B

stitch together Y and BP triangle; make 3 more units 2. Turn under seam allowance on **b** sides of all joined diamonds of unit 1 and press. Pin unit 1 to center of B square and neatly appliqué pressed edges in place with matching sewing thread. Stitch a unit 2 to each side of B square. Sew a B strip to each edge of block, mitering corners or overlapping ends as shown.

BLOCK A For each block cut a scant 5″ square from each of R, M, Y and GP. Cut each square in half diagonally to form two triangles. Following block diagram, stitch together triangles with ¼″ seams, first forming four squares of two triangles each, then joining four squares to form block, matching corners carefully. Make four A Blocks in all.

BLOCK B Cut a scant 5″ square from each of R, M, Y and GP. Cut each square in half diagonally to form two triangles. Following block diagram, stitch together triangles with ¼″ seams, first forming four squares of two triangles each, then joining four squares to form block. Make four B Blocks in all.

BLOCK C Cut eight Y squares, each a scant 1⅞″ on each side; cut nine BP squares same size. Cut a 2¼″ Y square; cut in half diagonally to form two small triangles. Cut a 3½″ Y square; cut in half diagonally to form two large triangles (use only one large triangle for each Block C square). From Y cut two rectangles 4″ by a scant 3¼″. From YP cut a scant 3¼″ square.

Following steps of assembly diagram and making ¼″ seams, stitch together a Y and a BP a square to form unit 1. Make seven more units 1. Stitch two small Y triangles to BP square to form unit 2. For step 2, stitch large Y triangle to unit 2 to form square. For step 3, stitch together two units 1 (note position of side Z) to form square. Make two more squares, following step 3. For step 4, stitch together the four

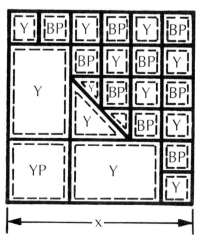

BLOCK C

ASSEMBLY FOR BLOCK C

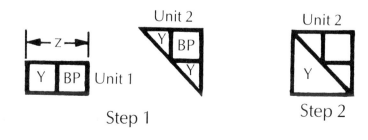

Step 1

Step 2

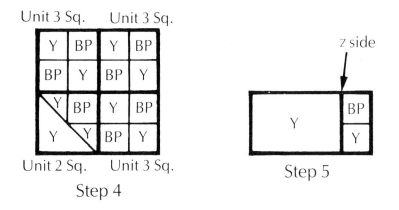

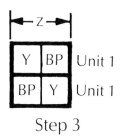

Step 3

Step 4

Step 5

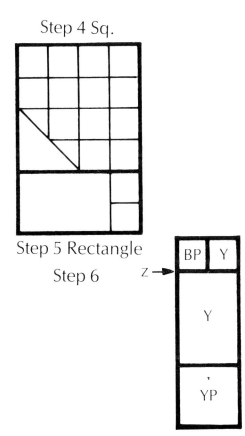

Step 4 Sq.

Step 5 Rectangle

Step 6

Step 7

squares made following steps 2 and 3. For step 5, stitch side Z of unit 1 to end of Y rectangle. For step 6, stitch rectangle (made in step 5) to lower edge of joined squares (step 4). For step 7, stitch unit 1 to end of Y rectangle as shown (note side Z) and YP square to other end of rectangle. Stitch this last strip (step 7) to side edge of other joined pieces (step 6) to complete block. Make twelve C Blocks in all.

BLOCK D From YP, cut a 4½″ square. From GP, cut a scant 5″ square; cut square in half diagonally to form two triangles. From B, cut an 8¾″ square; cut in half diagonally (use only one B triangle for each D block).

Following block diagram and making ¼″ seams, stitch GP triangles to adjoining sides of YP square as shown; stitch joined unit to B triangle along diagonal edges to form block. Make eight D Blocks in all.

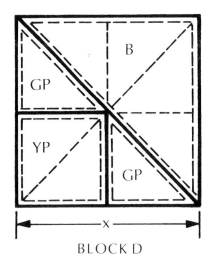

BLOCK D

BLOCK E Cut two scant 5″ squares each from B and GP. Cut each square in half diagonally to form two triangles. Following block diagram and making ¼″ seams, stitch together GP and B triangles along long sides to form four small squares. Stitch together four squares as shown to form block. Make four E Blocks in all.

HALF BLOCK F Enlarge pattern and cut it out from cardboard. Trace around the cardboard pattern on wrong side of YP, leaving at least ½″ between pieces. Cut out two of these parallelogram pieces. From BP, cut a 3⅛″ square and a 4½″ square; cut each square in half diagonally to form two triangles.

Following block diagram and making ¼″ seams, stitch a small and a large BP triangle to each YP parallelogram to form triangles as shown. Stitch these triangles together to form half block. Make eight F Half Blocks in all.

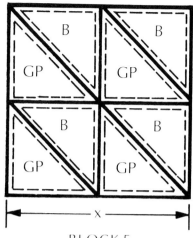

BLOCK E

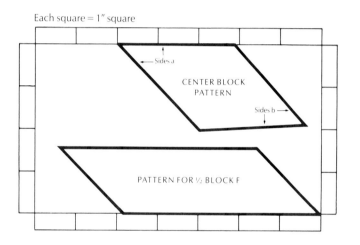

Each square = 1″ square

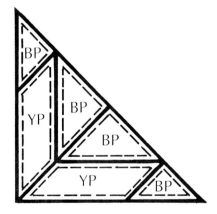

½ BLOCK F

BORDER SECTIONS On brown wrapping paper, make pattern, following measurements given on diagram. From RP, cut out eight border sections, adding ¼″ seam allowance all around.

With dressmaker's carbon paper, tracing wheel and yardstick, mark parallel quilting lines ½″ apart across each strip. See Placement Diagram for direction of lines.

BLOCK PLACEMENT DIAGRAM

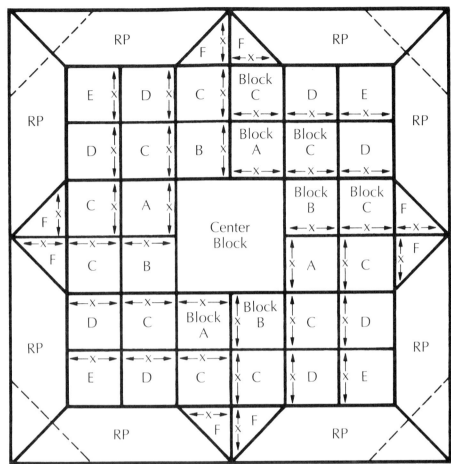

Dotted lines indicate directions of quilting lines on each quarter section.

TO ASSEMBLE TOP Carefully note which side of each block is the side X indicated on block diagrams; mark X side of your blocks with a pin or basting, if desired. Following Placement Diagram and placing X sides correctly, stitch blocks together with ¼″ seams, first making squares of four blocks each, then joining these squares to center block as follows: Join indicated three squares at top into a strip, then bottom three squares into a second strip, and center and adjoining blocks into a third; stitch three strips to each other, keeping positions correct and matching corners carefully. Stitch F Half Blocks together in pairs; join to border sections as shown to form border strip for each edge of quilt. Be sure, before joining, that quilting lines go in proper direction on each section. Stitch border strips to quilt; join corners (they will form miters).

TO ASSEMBLE QUILT Cut and piece YP to make lining 67" x 67" (1¼" larger all around than top). Cut quilt batt to about 1" larger all around than lining. Assemble top, batt and lining with batt centered in middle and top centered on batt and lining; baste layers together from top corners diagonally across to opposite lower corners, then across center from edge to edge in both directions.

TO QUILT Following directions that come with frame, mount quilt on frame. Working from the center outward, quilt tiny running stitches through all layers as follows: Following dotted lines on block diagrams for quilt lines, quilt blocks, working stitches about ¼" from seams on each section. Quilt marked lines on border strips.

FINISHING Trim batt to same size as quilt lining. To make and attach binding: From B, cut four 3¾" x 68" strips, piecing if necessary for length. With right sides together, making ¼" seams, center and sew a strip to each edge of quilt top, stitching to within ¼" of each end of edges (seams should meet at corners without crossing each other). Mitering corners and leaving 1½" showing on right side, turn excess fabric to wrong side; turn under ½" raw edges and stitch to quilt lining. Remove all basting threads.

PETIT SQUARES

A pieced coverlet by Barbara Rosen of Springfield, Missouri

Cottons, silk and synthetics blend together in an intricate geometric pattern inspired by an antique baby quilt, a winner from the 1870's.

about Barbara Rosen

Ten years ago, Barbara Rosen says she was so "haunted" by a quilt she saw on display in Kansas City — a single square surrounded by a border — that she "went back twice to look at it," and was finally compelled to sew a quilt that would also highlight a central square. She worked on her own magnificent piece off and on for several years, eventually finishing it off so that it could be hung. "I normally do not like patterns but this pattern is so tricky that it's fun," she explains. Rather than add a border, she continued the pieced design to fill out the spaces at the edge of the quilt. Although it is a complex and challenging quilt design, "it's easy to pick up and take with you," she says. "Stacks of the little squares can be cut and kept in egg cartons."

SIZE About 73″ x 89″.

MATERIALS One ½″-thick 81″ x 96″ polyester quilt batt; 45″-wide fabrics: 6⅝ yds. black velvet for lining and pieced squares, 3¼ yds. salmon satin, 2⅛ yds. total (or scraps) of pastel silks and satins in shades of lavender, yellow, cream, aqua, pink and green, 2 yds. total (or scraps) of embroidered decorative fabrics such as damask and taffeta or about 40 yds. total (or scraps) of 1″- to 1½″-wide embroidered ribbons; matching sewing threads; 2 (50-yd.) balls size 5 salmon pearl cotton for tufting; sharp, large-eyed needle.

BLOCKS See Assembly Diagram, Detail from Assembly Diagram, Individual Block Diagrams and Color Key. The pastel squares in each block are arranged to form diagonal color stripes when blocks are assembled.

Broken lines on Assembly Diagram indicate stripes, solid lines indicate blocks. See Detail Diagram, which shows four assembled blocks. Note that each block uses *three* pastel colors: the eight pastel squares around center black square are *one color* and the pastel squares at upper left and lower right corner are *shades of same color* because they are all within the same diagonal stripe; the three pastel squares at upper right corner are a *2nd color* because they are within another color stripe; and the pastel square at lower left corner

NOTE *Pieced quilt top is composed of 63 square blocks, 32 shaped border blocks and 4 shaped corner blocks. Each block is made by sewing small squares together. There is no quilting, but the velvet lining is tufted through to the center of each block.*

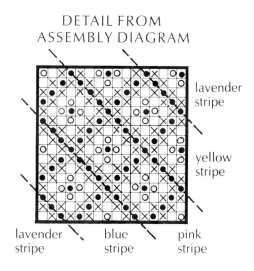

DETAIL FROM
ASSEMBLY DIAGRAM

lavender
stripe

yellow
stripe

lavender   blue   pink
stripe   stripe   stripe

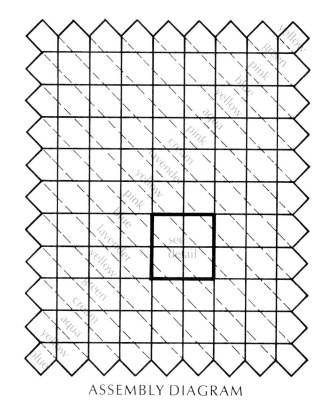

ASSEMBLY DIAGRAM

is a *3rd color*. Tag each block with a number as you complete it and mark the same number on the corresponding block on Assembly Diagram. This will help you to assemble blocks later in the correct color order.

Cut all pieces for blocks 1½″ square. When assembling them, sew ¼″ seams either by hand (this quilt was made entirely by hand) or by machine. Cut black velvet pieces from length of fabric, leaving two large sections for lining.

BLOCK A Cut 16 black velvet squares, 24 salmon squares, 8 embroidered squares (or cut eight 1½″ lengths of embroidered ribbons), 16 pastel squares (8 of one color, 2 of another shade of the same color, 2 of a 3rd shade of that same color, then 3 of a 2nd color and one of a 3rd color). Following Block A Diagram and Color Key, assemble squares as shown, sewing them into strips as follows: Hold 2 squares with right sides facing and sew together along one edge with ¼″ seam; sew strips together to form square block, matching corners carefully. Make 62 more Blocks A.

INDIVIDUAL BLOCK DIAGRAMS

upper left corner
Block I
(make 1)

upper edge
Block E
(make 7)

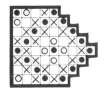

upper right corner
Block F
(make 1)

Color Key
⊠ Salmon
◯ Ribbon
⦿ Black
☐ Pastel

left edge
Block D
(make 9)

square
Block A
(make 63)

right edge
Block B
(make 9)

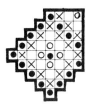

lower left corner
Block H
(make 1)

lower edge
Block C
(make 7)

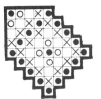

lower right corner
Block G
(make 1)

BLOCKS B through I For each block, cut squares as indicated in Individual Block Diagrams, placing pastel squares in color arrangement to fit diagonal stripe pattern.

TO COMPLETE TOP Following Assembly Diagram, sew blocks together, as follows, to form top: With right sides together, sew ¼" seams to join blocks in horizontal strips, then join strips to form top. To preserve puffy look, leave blocks unpressed.

TO ASSEMBLE QUILT Cut and piece velvet lining to same size as top; leave edge shaping for later. Assemble top, batt and lining with batt centered in middle. To facilitate handling, trim batt to size of lining. Baste layers together from top corners diagonally across to opposite lower corners, then across center from edge to edge in both directions. Pin edges, following outline of quilt top. Carefully cut lining and batt to shape of top, trimming batt slightly smaller. Turn in seam allowances and stitch edges together.

FINISHING Turn quilt wrong side up for tufting. Cut four 3" lengths of pearl cotton; thread into large-eyed needle. Insert needle through lining into a corner of center black velvet square on a block, then, taking a tiny stitch, bring needle back through corner to lining. Remove needle and tie threads in tight knot for a tuft. Make tuft in each of remaining three corners of same square. Make four tufts in the same way through center black square on each block. Remove all basting threads.

COTTON AND SATIN LACED QUILT

A comforter by Arleta Freeman of Marlow, Oklahoma

Here solid, print and satin fabrics are combined in an intriguing checkerboard pattern, systematically and easily executed by interlacing strips to create each block. Assembled top, batt and backing can be quilted either by machine (as this one was) or by hand.

about Arleta Freeman

Arleta Freeman's comforter grew out of her interest in home decorating and her desire to update her quilting skills, passed down through three generations. She wanted the homey look of a handsewn quilt, and was fascinated by the idea of lacing strips of fabric to produce a checkerboard effect. Because she wanted the spread "to be colorful and yet have a neutral color to set it together," she chose satins and cotton prints for the 8"-square blocks, and white satin to unite and unify the blocks. Beige eyelet squares join the corners of each block. Three layers of batting help "puff" each pattern block and square.

SIZE About 80″ x 90½″, finished.

MATERIALS Three ½″-thick 81″ x 96″ polyester quilt batts (number is optional; see NOTE at Padding, p. 46); one queen-sized white sheet for lining; 5½ yds. white muslin for background of blocks; 44″-wide satin: 4½ yds. white for separating bands and border, small amounts in many different colors for lacing; small amounts of cotton print fabrics in many different colors for lacing; 1 yd. pale beige cotton eyelet fabric for corner squares; matching sewing threads; ruler.

LACED BLOCKS For each block cut a 10″ muslin square for background. Cut eight 2″ x 9″ strips each from a colored satin and a printed cotton whose combined colors create a pleasing effect. Press ½″ raw edge to wrong side along each 9″ edge of each strip. Measure carefully, making sure pressed strip is exactly 1″ wide. Topstitch along each 9″ edge, sewing ⅛″ in from pressed edges.

Follow assembly diagram for the next steps. For step 1, with pencil and ruler mark line along top and right-hand side of muslin square 1″ in from edge. For step 2, place ends of eight satin strips over top marked line with long sides of each strip just touching (not overlapping) the strips next to it, and the top ½″ of the ends covering the marked line. (Center the group of strips, as in Diagram, so that 1″ of background square extends along each side.) Stitch top ends of strips in place, sewing along marked line.

In same manner, stitch ends of 8 cotton strips to line marked along side, being careful not to catch previously attached satin strips in stitching.

NOTE *Quilt is composed of fifty-six 8″-square blocks, each made separately of interlaced satin and cotton strips sewn to muslin squares. Blocks are joined to satin separating bands with eyelet square at each corner. Each block and square is padded. The top, batts (two used for this quilt) and lining are assembled, basted and quilted, and the border is then added.*

ASSEMBLY DIAGRAM

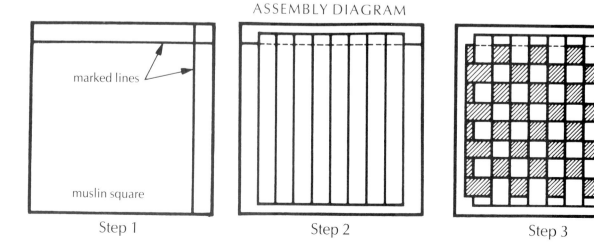

marked lines

muslin square

Step 1   Step 2   Step 3

For step 3, start at top right corner and weave first cotton strip over first satin strip, under next satin strip, over next, and so on, ending under last satin strip. Push cotton strip firmly against top sewing line and pull satin strips straight down to straighten weaving and form perfect 1″ squares. Throughout, be careful to keep all strips flat and untwisted. Pin ½″ leftover end of woven cotton strip in place at left side of muslin.

Weave second cotton strip "in reverse": under first satin strip, over next, under next, and so on, ending over last satin strip. Straighten weaving and pin end of cotton strip in place.

Continue weaving in this manner, forming checkerboard pattern. When weaving is completed, pin ends of satin strips along bottom edge as cotton strips have been pinned along left side. Stitch strip ends in place, sewing carefully, just along edge of last row of checkerboard squares, so as not to catch row in stitching.

Woven checkerboard area should measure 8″ square. Trim muslin square to 9″ square (this leaves ½″ all around woven area for seam allowance). Make 56 blocks in all, using a different color combination for each if you have enough different fabrics.

TO ASSEMBLE TOP Reserving enough fabric for border strips, from white satin, cut 127 satin bands, each 3½″ x 9″. From eyelet fabric, cut seventy-two 3½″ squares.

With right sides together, making ½″ seams, stitch a satin strip to top of each block, being careful not to catch woven area in seam; then join block units in seven vertical strips of eight blocks each separated by satin bands; stitch a satin band to bottom of strip.

With right sides together, making ½″ seams, stitch narrow end of each remaining satin band to side of an eyelet square; join band-square units in eight vertical strips of eight satin bands, each separated by a square; stitch a square to band at end of strip (9 squares on strip, with a square at each end.)

With right sides together, making ½″ seams and matching corners carefully, stitch together alternating block strips with strips of bands and squares to form top that is 7 blocks by 8 blocks with separating bands around each block.

Padding From one quilt batt, cut fifty-six 8″ squares and seventy-two 2½″ squares. Baste batt squares to wrong side of quilt top, putting one beneath each block and eyelet corner square. Padding gives quilt its extra fluffy look (see NOTE).

NOTE *On original quilt, in addition to padding for extra fluffiness, two quilt batts were used. For a quilt that is less thick, use only one batt.*

TO ASSEMBLE QUILT Cut sheet to make lining 80″ x 90½″ (or 1½″ larger all around than quilt top).

Assemble padded top, batt or batts and lining, with batt centered in middle and top centered on batt and lining; baste layers together from top corners diagonally across to opposite lower corners, then across center from edge to edge in both directions.

TO QUILT Original quilt was machine-stitched. If you feel it would be difficult for your machine to manage all the thicknesses, or you simply wish to quilt by hand, mount quilt on quilting frame (available at Sears and crafts stores), following mounting directions that come with frame. For either hand- or machine-stitching, work from center outward, making small stitches through all layers. Quilt around each block edge, stitching carefully right along seamline.

FINISHING Trim batt to same size as quilt lining. **Border** From white satin, cut two 5″ x 81″ strips and two 5″ x 90½″ strips (or 1″ longer than width and length of lining), piecing if necessary for length. With right sides together, making ½″ seams, center and stitch long strip to each long edge of quilt top. Leaving 2″ showing on right side, fold excess half of border strip to wrong side; turn under ½″ raw edges at ends and along quilt edge. Sew turned-under edge to lining. In same manner, stitch remaining strips to remaining edges of quilt top; fold in half to wrong side, covering ends of other border strips at corners; turn under raw edges and stitch in place. Remove all basting threads.

SHADED YO-YOS

A bedspread by Sandra Archbold of Dix Hills, New York

Radiant yo-yo bedspread is worked from the center out, with gathered circles of fabric added as you go.

about Sandra Archbold

Sandra Archbold calls her quilt her therapy. Between her own filled scrap bag and a friend's donation of old cottons from her grandmother's dry goods store, she decided it was time to plan a quilt. To cut the time in half and show up the fabrics better, she enlarged the standard yo-yo pattern (usually the size of a fifty-cent piece), using a pot cover as a pattern. She worked the first yo-yos in the evenings after her two babies were asleep. As they grew, she carried her materials, tucked in a cookie tin, to parks, playgrounds and doctors' offices. Her five-year-old daughter helped her sew and, when all the yo-yos were done, her toddlers helped sort and stack them by color. Sandra laid out the design and, when it looked "like sunshine and shadows" in her garden — light shades in the center radiating to dark shades at the edge — she knew the pattern was right.

NOTE *Spread is composed of 525 yo-yos, each 4¼" in diameter, in alternating rows of 10 and 11 across.*

SIZE About 68" x 106".

MATERIALS Assorted printed, plaid, checked, striped and solid-color cotton or cotton-blend fabrics in shades of white, yellow, light and dark blue, red and purple (¼ yard 45"-wide fabric will make 5 yo-yos, ¼ yard 36"-wide fabric will make 4 yo-yos); matching sewing threads.

TO MAKE A YO-YO Using 8¾"-diameter cardboard circle for pattern, cut fabric circle. Turn in edge ¼" and press, clipping so edge lies flat. Using two strands of thread, hand-sew running stitches around circle ⅛" from outer edge. With right side outward, pull threads tightly to form a hole ½" to ¾" wide; fasten off. Press flat with hole at center, forming 4¼"-diameter yo-yo.

TO ASSEMBLE To determine color placement, lay yo-yos on floor. Referring to photograph, start at center with predominantly white yo-yos, then proceed outward with predominantly yellow, light blue, red, dark blue and purple until the desired shape and color effect are achieved. Hand-sew adjacent edges of yo-yos together with the holes on the right side of the work.

ELVIS

A quilt by Sally Jean Brown of Elizabeth, Pennsylvania

Appliquéd lavishly in lamé and satin, this scintillating quilt is Sally Jean's homage to rock star Elvis Presley, whose hit songs are commemorated, like tender messages, in her dramatic border design.

about
Sally Jean Brown

He was "truly a great performer and that mainly was the inspiration for choosing the design," explains Sally Jean Brown, who won second prize in the contest for her spectacular appliqué design. The quilted "light rays," stitched on a purple satin background, luminously spotlight the starred central motif — unmistakably Elvis, right down to his bejewelled fingers and rhinestone-studded costume. In the border, trapunto song titles and appliquéd 45-rpm records emphasize the extraordinary talents of "the King of Rock and Roll." Sally Jean completed her quilt in twelve weeks, working on it every evening. She credits her mother-in-law, a seasoned needleworker, for invaluable advice about quilting, embroidery and sewing techniques.

NOTE *Quilt is composed of a large center panel with embroidered appliquéd design, joined to border panels with appliquéd and trapunto designs. Top, batt and lining are assembled and quilted, with final trim added last.*

Each square = 1″ square

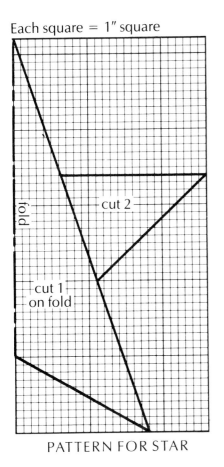

PATTERN FOR STAR

SIZE About 80″ x 83½″, finished. Quilt fits 60″-wide mattress with a 10″ overhang.

MATERIALS One ½″-thick 81″ x 96″ polyester quilt batt; 44″-wide satin: 5 yds. ecru for lining, 4 yds. blue, 4 yds. gold, 2 yds. black, 2 yds. red, ¼ yd. white; 1¾ yds. 36″-wide gold lamé; ½ yd. black percale; ¼ yd. flesh-colored crepe; ½ yd. good-quality cheesecloth; scrap of white plastic or textured fabric; 7½ yds. gold rickrack; soutache: 10 yds. black, 2 yds. gold; 1½ yds. gold and black piping; gold beads: 114 ¼″-long oblong, 61 ⅜″-diameter round and 50 ¼″-diameter round; a few other glass beads and rhinestones for jewelry; silver and gold metallic thread; cording: 10 yds. ¼″-diameter, 2 yds. ⅛″-diameter; silver metallic paint and fine brush; 6-strand embroidery floss, 1 skein each of black, flesh and pink; matching sewing threads; white quilting thread; dressmaker's carbon paper (in light or dark colors depending on fabric) and tracing wheel; ruler; quilting frame (available at Sears or craft stores).

CENTER (Elvis) PANEL From blue satin, cut two pieces, each 31″ x 64½″; join with ½″ seam along a 64½″ edge to form 61″ x 64½″ piece for background. From gold satin, cut two 11″ x 64½″ pieces for side border panels and two 11″ x 81″ pieces for top and foot border panels. Set border panels aside, reserving fabric scraps for appliqué below.

Enlarge Pattern for Star (see How to Enlarge Patterns, page 255). Cut pieces from gold lamé, adding ¼″ seam allowance. Fold under seam allowance and baste pieces to background, following Placement Diagram for position. Machine-topstitch ⅛″ in from all edges all around star; repeat ¼″ in from first stitching line.

Enlarge Elvis pattern pieces and remaining pieces on Placement Diagram (solid lines indicate pattern pieces; broken lines indicate quilting). Trace patterns onto right side of fabrics, leaving at least ½″ between pieces; use black satin for guitar, strap and hair, gold satin for guitar opening, red satin for trousers, jacket and cape; white satin for shirt; flesh crepe for face, hands and neck; black percale for shoe bottoms; white plastic for shoes. Cut out pieces, adding ¼″ seam allowance to all edges, except for plastic. Transfer embroidery details (on face, hands and guitar) and bead positions (on hands, chest, guitar and red satin clothes) to cut pieces with carbon paper. Following stitch diagrams, pages 238-242, embroider as many details as possible using satin stitch for eyebrows, lips and fingernails; outline stitch for eyes, cheeks, nose, fingers and name on guitar; couching

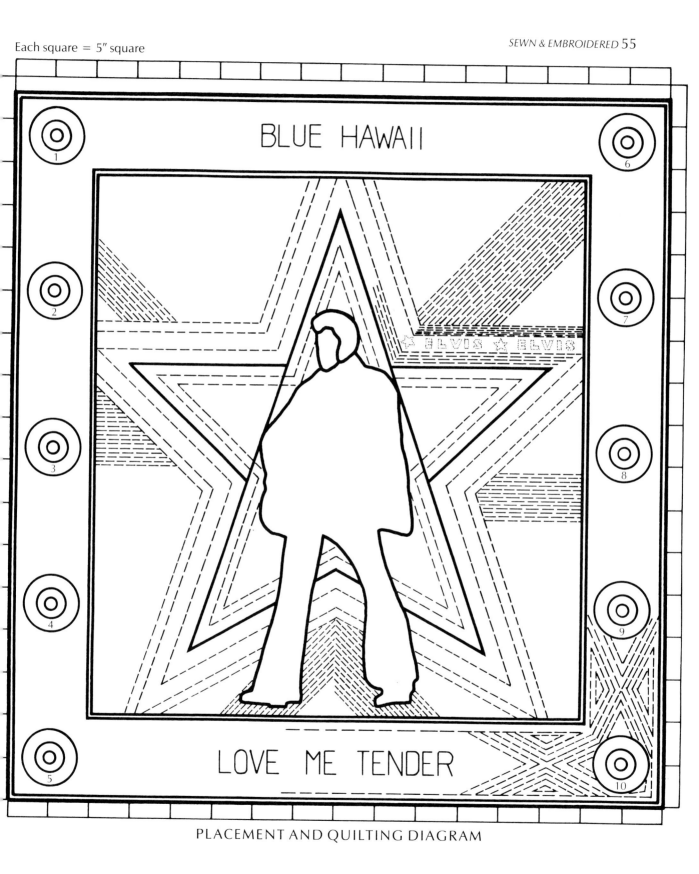

PLACEMENT AND QUILTING DIAGRAM

stitch for guitar strings. Securely attach beads (except for jewelry, explained in next paragraph). Any overlapping details can be added after pieces are appliquéd. Press under seam allowances, clipping seam allowance on curves.

Carefully pin or baste pieces in place, face piece first, then hair and shirt, then red clothes, then guitar. Pin raw edges of piping in position under guitar. With a narrow satin stitch and matching thread, machine-appliqué along pressed edges to fix pieces in place. Embroider any remaining details and sew on beads for rings and necklaces. Sew on gold soutache trim as indicated by narrow double lines.

BORDER PANELS Enlarge patterns for records from Placement Diagram. Tracing pattern onto fabric as before, use black satin for records, black percale for labels. Cut out, adding ¼″ seam allowance all around. With silver paint, carefully print in block letters a title on each record label. Titles used were ''Treat Me Nice'' (record 1), ''Don't Be Cruel'' (2), ''Heart Break Hotel'' (3), ''Jailhouse Rock'' (4), ''Blue Suede Shoes'' (5), ''It's Now or Never'' (6), ''Stuck on You'' (7), ''Hound Dog'' (8), ''All Shook Up'' (9) and ''That's All Right'' (10). Using backstitch (see Embroidery Stitches, page 238), outline letters with silver metallic thread. Press under seam allowance and machine-topstitch record pieces in place on border strips.

Following Placement Diagram for position, work song titles on top and foot panels as follows: Transfer or mark with basting threads position of lettering on panels (before marking fabric, read NOTE at Quilting Patterns, p.58). Cut two 5″ x 30″ strips of cheesecloth; baste to underside of border panels where letters are to be worked. (Work is done in trapunto; see page 237 if you are not familiar with this process.) With small running stitches through both satin and cheesecloth layers, sew two parallel lines ⅛″ apart in the shape of each block letter in turn. Thread narrow cord in tapestry needle; from underside (cheesecloth side), run needle with cording through the casing formed by the parallel quilting lines. Needle must be brought through cheesecloth at sharp curves and turns, then inserted again, leaving a small loop of yarn. Be careful not to draw cording through to top of quilt. With backstitch, outline letters, over quilting lines, with gold metallic thread.

ASSEMBLE TOP With ½″ seams, join side border panels to side edges of Center (Elvis) Panel; join top and foot border panels.

Each square = 2" square

ELVIS PATTERN

Note about pattern transfer
Because of fabrics used, top is not easily laundered. You may find it better to quilt "freehand," marking general placement of designs with pins, tailor's chalk or basting thread, than to use carbon paper for marking designs. Measure and work carefully. If you feel you need more exact guidelines to quilt, use a carbon paper in a color that contrasts only slightly with fabric for transferring designs.

QUILTING PATTERNS Transfer quilting designs if desired, or mark positions for designs following Placement and Quilting Diagram. See quilting instructions, below, for distances between lines.

TO ASSEMBLE QUILT Cut and piece together ecru satin to form lining piece same size as top. Cut quilt batt about 1″ larger all around than quilt top. Assemble three layers with batt in the middle and right (shiny) sides of top and lining both facing out; baste layers together from top corners diagonally across to opposite corners, then across center from edge to edge in both directions.

TO QUILT Following directions that come with frame, mount quilt on frame. Working from center outward, quilt tiny running stitches through all layers. Following Placement and Quilting Diagram, quilt as follows: Quilt 2 lines around inside of star 1″ and 2″ in from machine stitching. Quilt 4 lines ¼″ apart around outer edge of star. Quilt a line 2″ from last line around star. In 2″ space between lines just quilted, quilt star and ELVIS pattern, making both stars and letters 1½″ high. Quilt 5 more lines ⅛″ apart next to last star outline. Following positioning and directions on diagram, quilt parallel lines ½″ apart from star outline to edges of Elvis panel.

BORDER Quilt a circle ⅛″ from each record edge. Quilt lines ½″ apart, following pattern shown in Placement and Quilting Diagram.

FINISHING Cut 1½″-wide bias strips of red satin. Join bias strips and use to cover cording, making satin-covered cording piece long enough to fit all around quilt edge.

Trim batt ½″ smaller all around than top and lining fabrics. Turn in fabric edges; insert raw edges of covered cording between turned-in fabric edges, leaving only covered cording showing. Machine-topstitch close to turned edge all around quilt, catching all fabric layers. Topstitch a length of black soutache over stitching line.

Panel trim Cut 1″-wide bias strips of black satin. Join to form strip 250″ long. Press under ¼″ along each long edge, forming ½″-wide bias strip. Baste gold rickrack all around edge of Center (Elvis) Panel with outer edge just touching seam that joins border panels. Pin black bias strip over seam joining, covering only half of rickrack, the other half extending beyond the black strip. Miter strip corners and turn ends under. With gold metallic thread, machine-topstitch each side of bias strip.

LEVITTOWN

An appliquéd quilt by Gwen Evrard of Long Beach, New York

Snug and colorful little homes stand side by side with their quilted counterparts in this delightful, queen-sized coverlet, third prize winner in the contest.

about Gwen Evrard

Gwen Evrard's "tract" homes have to be the coziest ever! Each little house repeats the traditional school-house pattern, but has an unmistakable individuality, revealed in charming, personalized details—curtains, trees, shrubs, hanging plants, window boxes, "gingerbread" trim, shutters and more—all worked in embroidery stitches and appliqué. The alternating squares echo the outline of the house, quilted on muslin; the "wrong" side of the quilt comes up with its own interesting checkerboard, of muslin and colored cotton squares. Historically, these happy little houses represent the housing opportunities available to so many families in the post-war years—a time of hope and optimism that is well worth remembering today.

NOTE *Quilt is composed of 42 blocks: 21 are appliquéd and quilted, 21 are plain muslin and quilted. All blocks are made separately and stitched together, then the lining edges on each block are finished by hand. Each appliquéd block is lined with the same print used for sides of house and each plain block is lined with muslin so that the quilt back forms a checkerboard pattern.*

SIZE About 86″ x 100″, finished.

MATERIALS One ½″-thick 90″ x 108″ polyester quilt batt; 13½ yds. 45″-wide unbleached muslin; 1 yd. each of 7 different small-print cotton-blend fabrics for appliquéd houses and linings of appliquéd blocks; ¾ yd. moss-green fabric for grass strip below houses; 6-strand embroidery floss (see Embroidery and Color Key, p. 64, for stitches and colors) and scraps of printed fabrics, trims and laces for details; orange sewing thread for appliqués and quilting; white sewing thread to join blocks and borders; dressmaker's carbon paper and tracing wheel.

APPLIQUED BLOCK Cut 15″ square each from muslin, a printed fabric and batting. Cut 3″ x 15″ strip from green fabric for grass. Enlarge house pattern (see How to Enlarge Patterns, page 255), following solid lines (broken lines are for quilting). Cut out pattern pieces for house front and side, roof, windows, door and chimneys, adding ¼″ seam allowance to all edges.

Trace patterns for front and side of house on right side of same printed fabric as 15″ square; trace roof on another print, chimneys on a 3rd print or on scraps, windows and door on muslin. Before cutting out, use carbon paper and tracing wheel to mark quilting lines on pieces.

Turn under and press seam allowances on windows and

Each square = 1″ square

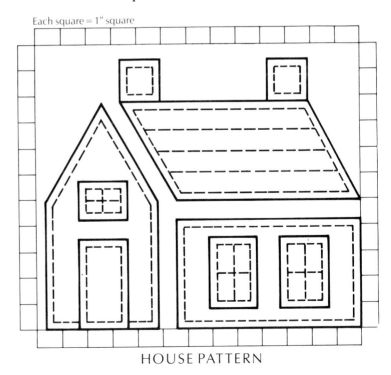

HOUSE PATTERN

door; appliqué to the house pieces, taking tiny vertical stitches.

For embroidery details, we have given an assortment of full-size motifs opposite the Embroidery and Color Key, below, for you to choose from; or you can make up your own details. Before appliquéing pieces to muslin square, transfer details to pieces with carbon paper, using tracing wheel or stylus such as empty cartridge from ballpoint pen. Following stitch diagrams, pages 238-242, embroider as many details as possible, then apply laces and trims for curtains, shutters, etc. Any overlapping details can be added after base pieces have been appliquéd.

Turn under and press one long edge of grass strip and all edges of house pieces except lower edges of house front and side. Match and pin ends and long raw edge of grass strip to bottom edge of muslin square. Pin house pieces in place, sliding seam allowance at lower edges of house front and side under folded edge of grass. Appliqué all pressed edges. Embroider additional details.

Baste appliquéd top, batt and lining together from top corners diagonally across to opposite lower corners. Following quilting lines, quilt tiny running stitches through all layers.

PLAIN QUILTED BLOCK Cut two 15″ squares from muslin and one from batting. Using tracing wheel and light-colored carbon paper, transfer full-size house pattern to one muslin square, following solid and broken lines. Baste together all three layers. Quilt all lines, stopping ½″ from edges of block.

TO ASSEMBLE BLOCKS (after you have planned their arrangement): Hold 2 blocks with right sides together; making ½″ seam, stitch adjacent edges together, stitching through top square and batting only (lining will be finished by hand). Trim batting at seamline to about ¼″. Stitch blocks together in this manner to form horizontal or vertical strips, then stitch strips together to form quilt top. To finish edges of lining squares, turn under one seam allowance and lap it over seam allowance on adjacent block; stitch down. Finish all raw edges in this manner except those on outer edges of quilt.

BORDER Cut 4″-wide strips of muslin and piece to fit one edge of quilt. With right sides together and edges matching,

stitch strip to quilt edge through all thicknesses. Fold in half to wrong side, turn under raw edge and stitch. Stitch borders on opposite edge of quilt, then on the two ends, cutting the end borders 1″ longer than quilt width, turning ends in ½″ and stitching them down. Quilt a straight line ½″ in from each edge. Quilt around each block ½″ in from seams. Remove all basting threads.

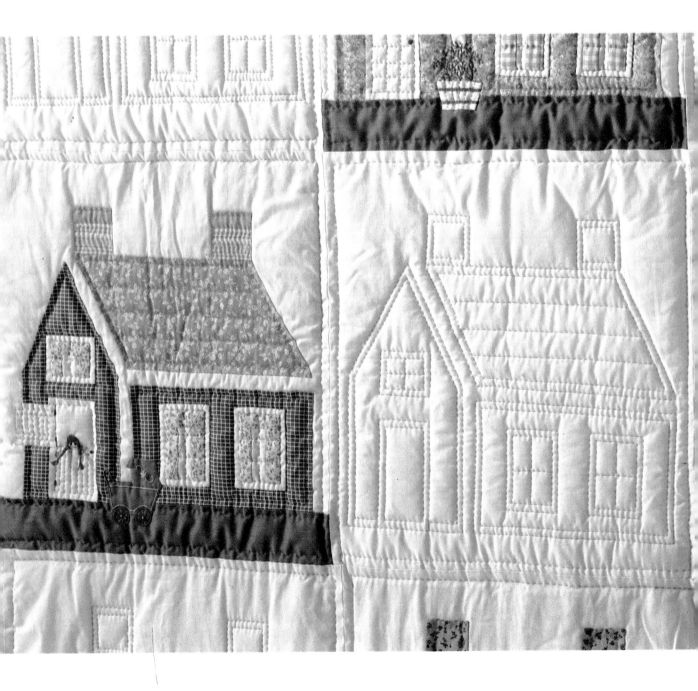

EMBROIDERY AND COLOR KEY

Use 2 strands of floss throughout. For embroidery stitch diagrams, see page 238.

Container of flowers *Container:* denim appliqué. *Stems and leaves:* green outline and lazy-daisy stitches. *Flowers:* salmon lazy daisies with brown French-knot centers, yellow star-stitch flowers. *Circles:* blue satin stitch. *Blue flower on container:* lazy-daisy and outline.

Eagle Black satin stitch.

Baby carriage *Carriage:* rust appliqué. *Inner line:* blue outline stitch. *Flower:* blue outline and lazy-daisy stitches. *Handle:* brown and blue outline stitch. *Wheels:* brown outline stitch with blue French-knot axles.

Door basket *Basket:* brown appliqué with brown couched straight stitches. *Stems and leaves:* green outline and lazy-daisy stitches. *Flowers:* yellow and orange star stitch and lazy daisies. *Dots:* brown and orange French knots.

Bird *Body:* brown satin stitch. *Bill and leg:* yellow straight stitches. *Eye:* black French knot.

Tree *Trunk and branches:* brown long-and-short stitches. *Twigs:* brown outline stitch.

Flower pot *Pot:* brown satin stitch. *Stems:* green outline stitch. *Flowers:* orange lazy daisies.

Bell Black satin and outline stitches.

Bike *Frame:* 2 rows red outline stitch. *Wheels:* 2 rows gray outline stitch for tires, 1 row for spokes.

Hanging sign *Sign:* brown appliqué. *Inner lines:* blue and orange outline stitch. *Initial* (make your own): pink outline stitch. *Flower:* blue lazy daisy. *Hanger:* brown outline stitch.

Girl's head *Braids:* free swinging and made of braided brown floss tied with orange ties. *Top of head and bangs:* brown satin stitch. *Features:* outline stitch pink chin and orange mouth, pink French-knot cheeks, black French-knot eyes. *Hands:* pink satin stitch.

Corn *Leaves:* tan and beige long-and-short stitch. *Corn:* yellow, wine and rust satin-stitch sections.

Pumpkin *Sections:* orange satin stitch separated by outline stitch. *Stem:* green outline stitch.

Jack-o'-lantern *Pumpkin:* Orange satin stitch. *Stem:* green outline stitch. *Face:* brown outline-stitch mouth, French-knot eyes and nose.

Weather vane Gray satin and outline stitches.

Flag *Background:* white and blue appliqué. *Stars:* tiny white straight stitches. *Each red stripe:* 2 rows outline stitch. *Pole:* 2 rows brown outline stitch. *Knobs:* brown and gray satin stitch.

Hanging basket *Basket:* brown satin stitch. *Vines:* green outline stitch. *Flowers:* pink lazy daisies.

Flower border *Stems and leaves:* medium and light green outline and lazy-daisy stitch. *Flowers:* orange and yellow star stitch. Repeat border to desired length.

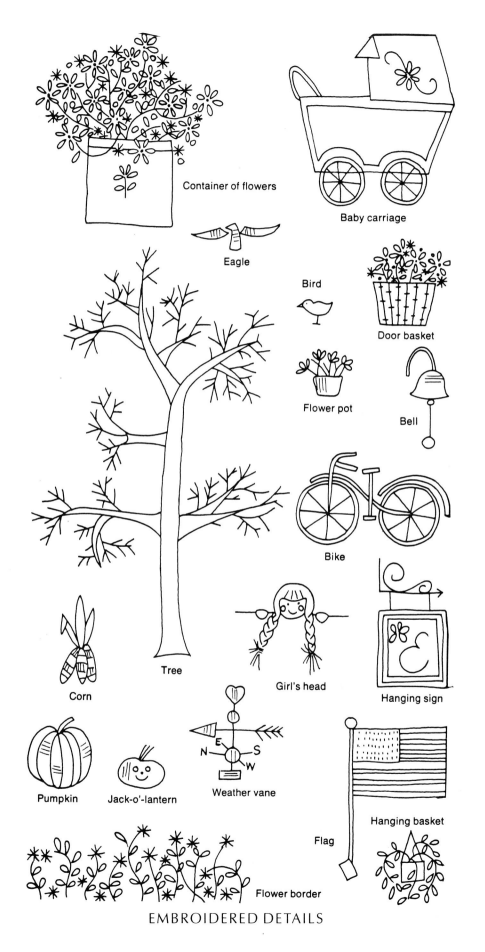

Container of flowers

Baby carriage

Eagle

Bird

Door basket

Flower pot

Bell

Tree

Bike

Corn

Girl's head

Hanging sign

Pumpkin

Jack-o'-lantern

Weather vane

N E S W

Hanging basket

Flag

Flower border

EMBROIDERED DETAILS

AUTUMN HARVEST

An appliquéd quilt by Grace Stinton of Auburn, Michigan

The crisp but muted shades of the glorious autumn season are celebrated in this bountiful harvest of bright orange pumpkins, cheery yellow flowers, lively blue buds and leaves in subtle shades of green — all appliquéd, in twenty-four blocks, onto an earthy background.

about Grace Stinton

Grace Stinton's big old farmhouse in Michigan is surrounded, in the fall, by fields of pumpkins — a dazzling sight that made her yearn, for years, to design a quilt that would glow with the same splendor. The random pattern of the pumpkins in the field grew more formal in her design, but she feels this design is "more pleasing to the eye" than her original idea would have been. The mother of nine children, Grace learned her sewing skills from her 90-year-old mother-in-law. Like all of Grace's projects, the pumpkin quilt spanned several seasons — piecing in the winter and quilting in warmer weather, work at the quilting frame being much more comfortable in an unheated "summer kitchen."

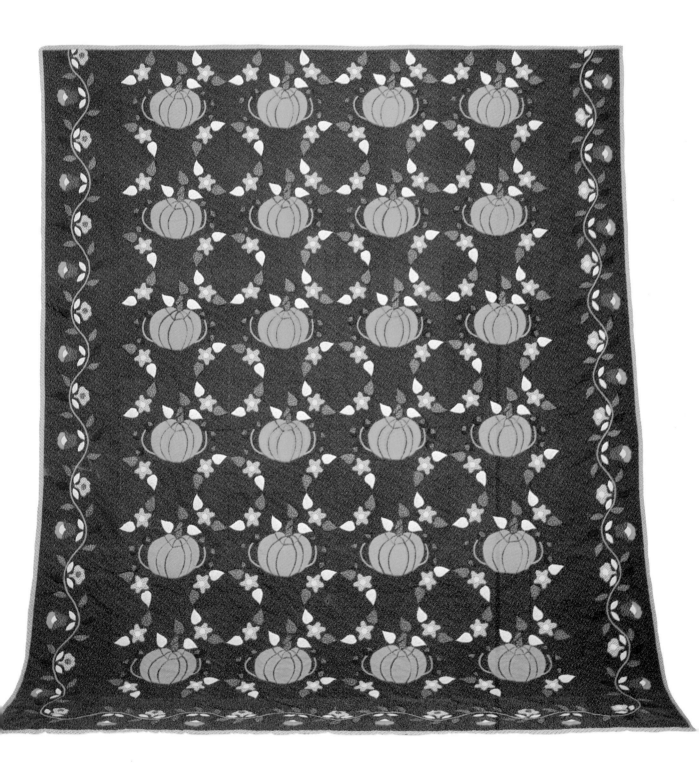

NOTE *Quilt is composed of twenty-four 18"-square blocks which form center panel 4 blocks wide by 6 blocks long. Quilt can be made smaller by omitting a strip of blocks in either or both directions; if the latter, finished quilt will measure 81" x 104½". Each block top is appliquéd separately, then blocks are joined to form panel. Borders with appliquéd designs are added to sides and bottom. Top, batt and lining are then basted together and quilted; edges are bound.*

SIZE About 99" x 122½", finished.

MATERIALS Two ½"-thick 81" x 96" polyester quilt batts; two extra-long twin-size sheets or 10½ yds. percale in brown for lining; 36"-wide solid color or small-design print percale: 13½ yds. brown print (BP) for background, 2 yds. orange (O), 1½ yds. mustard print for binding, 1 yd. each of pale green print (PG), medium green print (MG) and dark green print (DG), ½ yd. each of blue print (B), brick red print (R) and bright yellow print (YP), ¼ yd. plain yellow (Y); matching sewing threads; bright orange quilting thread; four 5-yd. packages green single-fold bias tape; dressmaker's carbon paper and tracing wheel; quilting frame (available at Sears or craft stores).

APPLIQUÉD BLOCKS Reserving enough fabric for border strips (see below), cut twenty-four 19" squares from brown print (½" seam allowance included). Enlarge patterns (see How to Enlarge Patterns, page 255). Trace patterns on right side of fabrics, following color key and leaving at least ½" between pieces. Cut pieces from fabric, adding ¼" seam allowance all around.

Turn under and press seam allowances, clipping them on curves. Following Block Diagram for position, pin pieces in place, using bias tape for vine stems. Appliqué all pressed edges, matching thread color to fabric. Make 24 in all.

TO ASSEMBLE TOP Stitch squares together in 4 vertical or 6 horizontal strips with ½" seams. Stitch strips together, matching block corners, to make center panel 4 blocks wide by 6 blocks long, or size desired.

BORDERS From brown print, cut a 13½" strip the width of panel; with ½" seam, join to lower edge of center panel. Also from brown print, cut two 13½" strips the length of panel with attached border; with ½" seams, stitch a strip to each side edge of panel and border strip. (Border spans three edges only — bottom, and left and right sides.)

Enlarge border patterns. Trace, cut out from fabrics and press under seam allowance in same manner as for Appliquéd Blocks. Following Border Diagram for placement, pin corner motifs in place, then repeat section indicated across bottom, having 6 red-orange flowers between corner motifs. Space flowers evenly across, adjusting bias tape vine stem as needed to fit. In same manner, repeat border section up each side edge, having 8 or 9 red-orange flowers evenly spaced between corner motif and top edge. Appliqué all pressed edges, matching thread color to fabric.

Each square = 1″ square

BLOCK DIAGRAM

TO ASSEMBLE QUILT Cut and piece sheets or brown percale to make lining 99″ x 122½″ (or other size, if different). Cut and piece quilt batts (lap edges ½″ and topstitch) to about 1″ larger all around than lining. Assemble top, batt and lining with batt centered in the middle and top centered on batt and lining; baste layers together from top corners diagonally across to opposite lower corners, then across center from edge to edge in both directions.

TO QUILT Following directions that come with frame, mount quilt on frame. Working from the center outward, quilt tiny running stitches through all layers. Quilt around outside edge of each appliquéd piece.

FINISHING Trim batt to same size as quilt lining. **Binding** From mustard print, cut two strips 3″ x 100″ (or actual length), piecing as necessary for length. With right sides together, making ½″ seams, center and stitch strips to top and bottom of quilt top, leaving ½″ extended at each end of strip. Leaving 1″ showing on right side, turn excess width of binding strip fabric to wrong side; turn under ½″ raw edge and stitch to quilt lining. From mustard print, cut and piece two strips 3″ x 123½″ (or needed length). In same manner as before, bind each side edge of quilt, folding in and sewing excess fabric to miter corners. Remove all basting threads.

Each square = 1" square

Y on right side,
B on left and bottom

DG on sides
MG on bottom

Y on right side,
B on left and bottom

DG on sides
MG on bottom

BP

BORDER DIAGRAM

ALASKAN BABY QUILT

A coverlet by Pamela D. Joseph of Gaithersburg, Maryland

Six superb outdoor scenes, each a picturesque slice of Alaskan life, rekindle the frontier spirit as they keep a new baby warm.

about Pamela D. Joseph

Pamela Joseph drew on family recollections of Alaska for motifs in designing her baby coverlet. Each panel tells its own story about the vast state where she and her husband spent several years, and where her niece, a true Alaskan, was born. Made as a gift for this baby, the quilt is a warm reminder of her unique birthplace. At top left, Mt. KcKinley rises up into a sky ablaze with the Northern Lights; at top right, an Eskimo concentrates on ice-fishing, a way of life on the North Slope; panning for gold (left center) recalls the lure of Alaska before the oil boom; a Russian Orthodox church (right center) symbolizes the Russian influence in Alaska; a log cabin homestead (bottom left) portrays the freedom to claim a piece of land, settle on it and cultivate it. At lower right, a whale, polar bear and bald eagle stand for Alaska's wildlife.

SIZE About 29″ x 48″, finished.

MATERIALS One ½″-thick 81″ x 96″ polyester quilt batt; cotton-blend fabric: 4 yds. bright yellow (BY), 1½ yds. bright green (BG), 1¼ yds. sky blue (SB), ½ yd. pale green (PG), ¼ yd. each of mint green (MG), dark green (DG), pale blue (PB), royal blue (RB), navy blue (NB), purple (P), orange (O), red (R), white (W), brown (BR), tan (T) and black (BK); matching sewing thread; 6-strand embroidery floss, 1 skein each of brown, tan, pink, bright and dark blue, pale, medium and dark green; green quilting thread; dressmaker's carbon paper and tracing wheel; quilting frame (available at Sears or craft stores).

APPLIQUÉD BLOCKS Cut five 10½″ x 13″ rectangles from sky blue fabric and one the same size from pale green for block backgrounds (green is for Prospector Block). A ½″ seam allowance is included. Enlarge pattern (see How to Enlarge Patterns, page 255). Using solid lines on patterns for outline (dotted lines indicate embroidery details), trace patterns on right side of fabric, following color key and leaving at least ½″ between pieces. Cut out pieces from fabric, adding ¼″ seam allowance all around.

NOTE *Quilt is composed of six 9½″ x 12″ blocks, separating bands and borders. Each block top is made separately (appliquéd and embroidered), then blocks are joined to bands. Top, batt and lining are assembled and quilted, then finished with added border.*

Turn under and press seam allowances, clipping them on curves. Following each Block Diagram for placement, appliqué pieces in place as follows: Beginning with large underlying pieces (e.g., mountains, grass, water), pin pieces in place. Matching thread color to fabric, appliqué all pressed edges. (Edges that will be concealed can be left unturned and free; this avoids the possibility of a ridge. The overlapping layer will fasten the lower one down.) Repeat with each succeeding layer, working small details last. Embroider details such as tent ropes, fishing line and small trees behind homestead with 3 strands of embroidery floss.

Each square = 1" square

TENT BLOCK DIAGRAM

Each square = 1" square

PROSPECTOR BLOCK DIAGRAM

Each square = 1" square

HOMESTEAD BLOCK DIAGRAM

Each square = 1" square

ESKIMO BLOCK DIAGRAM

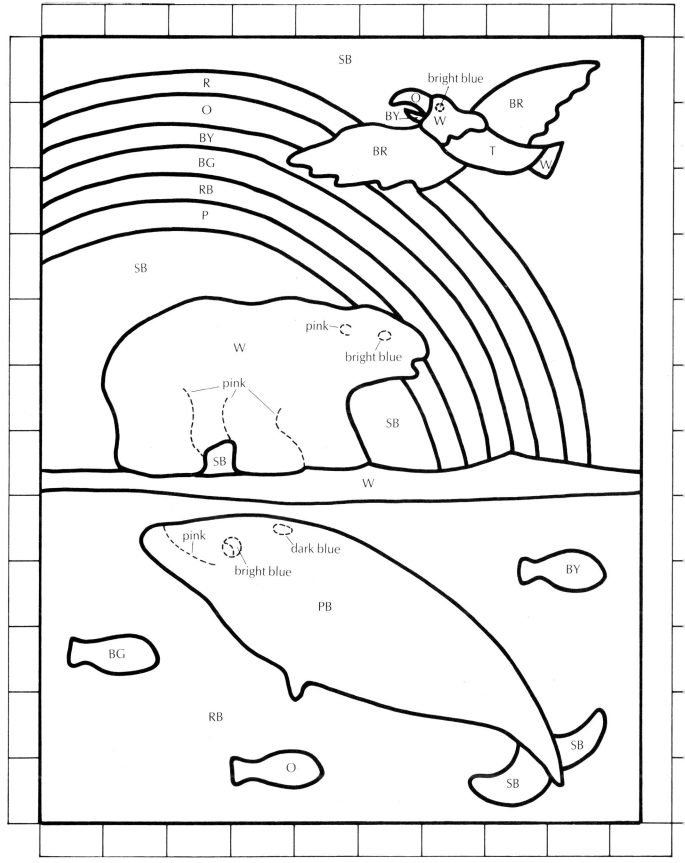

Each square = 1" square

WILDLIFE DIAGRAM

CHURCH BLOCK DIAGRAM

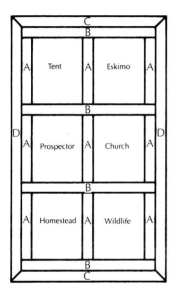

PLACEMENT DIAGRAM

TO ASSEMBLE TOP: Bands From bright yellow fabric, cut nine strips each 3″ x 13″ (A band) and four strips each 3″ x 26″ (B band). Following Placement Diagram for position, join as follows: With right sides together and making ½″ seams, stitch an A band to left side of Tent Block, stitch another A band to right side of Tent Block. Stitch left side of Eskimo Block to opposite side of last A band; stitch another A band to right side of Eskimo Block, forming a strip. Stitch B bands to top and bottom edges of just-joined strip. In same manner, form strip of A band, Prospector Block, A band, Church Block and A band; join top edge of new strip to lower edge of last B band, carefully aligning strip to correspond to first strip. Stitch another B band to lower edge of new strip. Join A band, Homestead Block, A band, Wildlife Block and A band; join top edge of new strip to lower edge of last B band. Stitch another B band to botttom edge of strip to form panel 26″ x 45″.

TO ASSEMBLE QUILT Cut and piece bright yellow fabric to form lining 29″ x 48″. Cut quilt batt about 1″ larger all around than lining. Assemble top, batt and lining with batt centered in middle and top panel centered on batt and lining. Baste layers together from top corners diagonally across to opposite lower corners, then across center from edge to edge in both directions.

TO QUILT Following directions that come with frame, mount quilt on frame. Working from center out, quilt tiny running stitches through all layers. Quilt around each block just inside edge (note, in Homestead Block, quilting lines across cabin). Quilt around edge of each appliquéd shape very close to pressed edge.

FINISHING Trim batt to same size as quilt lining. **Borders** From bright green, cut two 5″ x 31″ strips (C in diagram) and two 5″ x 50″ strips (D in diagram). With right sides together, making ½″ seams, center and stitch a D strip to each long side of quilt, sewing to within last ½″ at top and bottom of panel. In same manner, join C strips to top and bottom edges. (Seamlines should meet at corners without crossing over.) Smooth border strips out to edge of quilt lining, mitering corners; leaving 2″ border showing on right side, fold excess border fabric to wrong side over lining; pin along folded edge. Turning the raw edges under ½″ and mitering corners, stitch corners and stitch border edge to lining. Remove all basting threads.

TWISTED RIBBONS

A bridal quilt by Jane Soulant of New Orleans, Louisiana

This gift from mother to daughter, exquisitely hand-quilted, renders the theme of love with ribbons twisting in unbroken circles and classic hearts and flowers.

about Jane Soulant

Wedding symbols abound in Jane Soulant's prize-winning quilt, every motif a salute to that happiest of events, her daughter's marriage. Inspired by the song, ''Scarlet Ribbons,'' one of her daughter's favorites, Jane designed her twisted ribbon motif (originally thirty-seven patches of fabric sewn together in a block; here carried out with appliquéd ribbon). After piecing the quilt top by machine (''The sewing machine enables me to finish a top faster; I relax with the hand quilting''), she set to work on embellishments — predominantly, and not surprisingly, hearts and flowers. An experienced seamstress who taught herself quilting, Jane now likes ''to have two quilts going at once, one on the machine and one to be quilted, so I can work on whichever I like at the moment.''

SIZE About 102" x 116", finished.

MATERIALS Two ½"-thick 81" x 96" polyester quilt batts; 14 yds. 45"-wide unbleached muslin; 8½ yds. 45"-wide printed striped fabric (fabric should alternate light and dark stripes); sewing thread to match printed fabric; white quilting thread; dressmaker's carbon paper and tracing wheel; sheet of 8- or 10-to-the-inch graph paper; quilting frame (available at Sears or craft stores).

BLOCK The blocks on the original quilt were pieced in strips. Without changing the look of the quilt, we have adapted the design to the simpler appliqué method.

Following Patterns and Placement Diagram, draw the 4 solid-line shapes to size on graph paper and cut out. (Broken-line shapes are repeats of solid-line shapes; dotted-line shapes indicate quilting.) Cut a 15" square from muslin.

NOTE *Quilt is composed of thirty 14"-square blocks that form center panel 5 blocks wide by 6 blocks long. Quilt can be made narrower by omitting one 6-block strip. Each block top is appliquéd separately, then blocks are joined to form panel. Borders are added, corners mitered. Top, batt and lining are then basted together and quilted.*

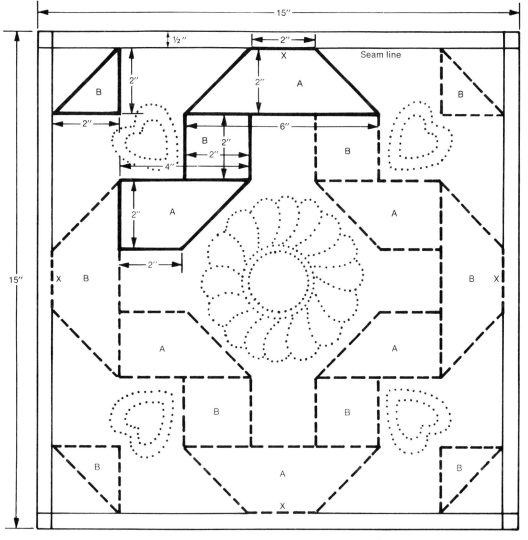

PATTERNS AND PLACEMENT DIAGRAM

Mark ½″ seam allowance *inside* each edge. Trace patterns on right side of printed fabric, centering and tracing patterns marked A on light-colored stripes and patterns marked B on dark stripes (see photograph for A and B stripe directions), being sure to leave at least ½″ between pieces. Cut out pieces, adding ¼″ seam allowance to all edges.

Matching marked seamlines, stitch together all pieces except triangles to form twisted-ribbon motif. Turn under and press all outer and inner edges of motif and edges of triangles. Pin motif to center of muslin square and triangles to corners, placing edges X of motif and outer corners of triangles at seamlines of square. Appliqué in place with tiny invisible stitches.

TO ASSEMBLE TOP Stitch completed squares together in vertical or horizontal strips, carefully matching light print to dark at each X on adjacent squares. Stitch strips together.

Inner printed border Cut 3″-wide strips from dark stripes, piecing to make one strip 5″ longer than one edge of center panel. With right sides together and edges matching, center strip along edge of panel; stitch. Make and attach borders to remaining 3 edges of panel, mitering corners. Trim mitered corner seams to ½″.

Wide muslin border Cut 11″-wide muslin strips, piecing to make one strip 22″ longer than one edge on quilt. Center and stitch to edge. Make and attach borders to remaining 3 edges, following same procedure. Miter corners.

Outer print border Work as for other borders, cutting print strips 6″ wide and piecing to make strips 11″ longer than each edge of quilt.

QUILTING PATTERNS Enlarge quilting patterns (see How to Enlarge Patterns, page 255), and transfer to quilt top as follows: Use yellow or light blue dressmaker's carbon paper and tracing wheel. Transfer flower to center of each square and small heart to each corner. Transfer corner motif over each mitered corner seam on muslin border. Transfer feather-and-medallion motif to muslin border at top and bottom of quilt, then transfer one or two small hearts to center of medallions or lightly draw your initials in script. Transfer feather-and-heart motif along each muslin side border.

TO ASSEMBLE QUILT Cut and piece quilt batts (lap edges ½″ and topstitch) to about 1″ larger all around than quilt top. Cut and piece muslin lining to same size as top.

QUILTED BLOCK MOTIF

Assemble the 3 layers, batt in the middle; baste together from top corners diagonally to opposite lower corners, then across center from edge to edge in both directions.

TO QUILT Following directions that come with frame, mount quilt on frame. Working from center outward, quilt tiny running stitches through all layers. Quilt all marked motifs, just outside all edges of twisted ribbon motifs, around inner print border and along edge where muslin and outer border join.

FINISHING Trim batt ½″ smaller all around than fabric. Turn in fabric edges and slipstitch. Quilt straight line 1″ in from each edge.

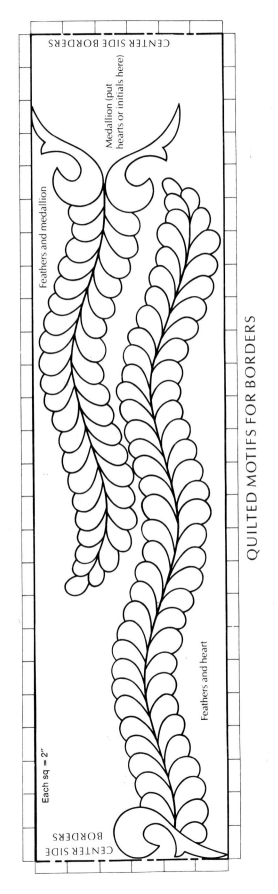

QUILTED MOTIFS FOR BORDERS

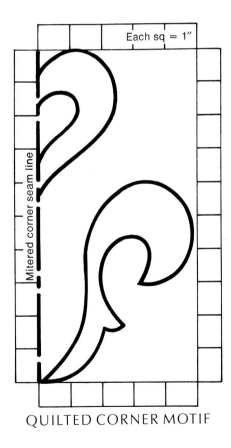

Each sq = 1″

Mitered corner seam line

QUILTED CORNER MOTIF

LANDSCAPE SCENES

An appliquéd quilt by Rhue T. Luna of Hemet, California

Six appliquéd scenes are worked separately in blocks and then arranged symmetrically around a seventh scenic panel to create this lively decorative quilt.

about Rhue T. Luna

Rhue Luna's love of painting outdoor scenery translates perfectly into playful experimentation with appliqué "compositions" — each one her own very original design. Using simple shapes that would be easy to sew, she let her imagination sail, first sketching out ideas for each block and then drawing them to size on newspaper with a large felt-tip pen. She cut out each shape and used it as her pattern piece, allowing a ¼" seam allowance all around. Going back to the scenes she had drawn, Rhue decided that plain cotton colors would best bring out her designs; most of them she found right in her scrap bag. Except for the trim around each scene, the entire quilt is handsewn.

SIZE About 50″ x 69″, finished.

MATERIALS One ½″-thick 81″ x 96″ polyester quilt batt; cotton-blend fabric, 36″-wide: 5 yds. brown (BR) for lining and appliqué, 2½ yds. dark brown (DB) for borders and appliqué; 1¼ yds. each of violet (V), turquoise (TB), light blue (LB) and forest green (FG); ¾ yds. deep blue (B), ½ yd. each of white (W), red (R), baby blue (BB), navy (N), avocado (A) and pea green (PG); ¼ yd. each of black (BK), pale yellow (PY), yellow (Y), gold (G), mustard (M), orange (O), burnt orange (BO), burgundy (BU), rust (RS), pink (P), dark avocado (DA) (or olive), tan (T), gray (GY) and dark gray (DG); matching sewing threads; ¾ yds. black piping for butterfly (this is optional); dressmaker's carbon paper and tracing wheel; ruler; quilting frame (available at Sears or craft stores).

NOTE *Quilt is composed of seven blocks of varying sizes, separating bands and borders. Each block top is appliquéd separately, then blocks are joined to bands. Top, batt and lining are assembled and quilted, then finished with added border.*

APPLIQUÉD BLOCKS (for background): From violet fabric, cut one rectangle 16″ x 23″ (Sailboat Block) and another 11″ x 32″ (Canyon Block); from turquoise, cut 2 rectangles each 16″ x 23″ (Orchard and Barn Blocks); from baby blue, cut one rectangle 11″ x 32″ (Waterfalls Block); from light blue, cut one rectangle 23″ x 32″ (Rainbow Block) and another 16″ x 23″ (Pier Block). A ½″ seam allowance is included for each block.

To appliqué Enlarge patterns for each block (see How to Enlarge Patterns, page 255). Use solid lines on patterns for outline (broken lines are for quilting). Trace patterns on right side of fabrics, following color key and leaving at least ½″ between pieces. On large pieces to be quilted, such as hills or grass, mark quilting lines on pieces, using carbon paper, tracing wheel and ruler for straight lines, before cutting out. Also mark quilting lines in sky areas on background pieces. Cut appliqué pieces from fabric, adding ¼″ seam allowance all around.

Turn under and press seam allowances, clipping them on curves. Following each Block Diagram for position, appliqué pieces in place as follows: Beginning with large underlying pieces (e.g., hills, grass, water), pin pieces in place. Matching thread color to fabric, appliqué all pressed edges. (Edges that will be concealed can be left unturned and free; this avoids the possibility of a ridge. The overlapping layer will fasten the lower one down.) Repeat with each succeeding layer, working small details last.

RAINBOW BLOCK DIAGRAM

TO ASSEMBLE TOP (bands): From dark brown, cut two 3″ x 16″ strips (band A), two 3″ x 32″ strips (band B) and two 3″ x 47″ strips (band C). Following Placement Diagram for position, join as follows: With right sides together and making ½″ seams, stitch one A band to right edge of Sailboat Block; stitch left edge of Orchard Block to opposite side of this band A, forming strip. Sew one band C to lower edge of strip. In same manner, form another strip composed of Waterfalls Block, band B, Rainbow Block, band B and Canyon Block; attach top edge of this strip to lower edge of first band C; attach second band C to lower edge of new strip. In same manner, form another strip consisting of Barn Block, band A and Pier Block; attach to lower edge of second band C to form top panel measuring 47″ x 66″.

TO ASSEMBLE QUILT Cut and piece brown fabric to form lining 50″ x 69″. Cut quilt batt about 1″ larger all around than lining. Assemble top, batt and lining with batt centered in middle and top panel centered on batt and lining. Baste layers together from top corners diagonally across to opposite lower corners, then across center from edge to edge in both directions.

TO QUILT Following directions that come with frame, mount quilt on frame. Working from the center out, quilt tiny running stitches through all layers. Quilt around each appliquéd piece, making one row of stitches ⅛″ *outside* pressed edge and one row ⅛″ *inside* the edge. Quilt additional lines marked on individual diagrams — on backgrounds, large pieces and such surrounding pieces as clouds, treetops, etc. Quilt around each block ⅛″ from border strips.

FINISHING Trim batt to same size as quilt lining. **Borders** From dark brown, cut two 5″ x 51″ strips (D in diagram) and two 5″ x 70″ strips (E in diagram). With right sides together and making ½″ seams, center and stitch a long strip (E) to each long side of quilt, sewing to within last ½″ at top and bottom. In same manner, join remaining strips (D) to top and bottom edges. (Seamlines should just meet at corners without crossing over.) Smooth border strips out to edge of quilt lining, mitering corners; leaving 2″ border showing on right side, fold excess border fabric to wrong side over lining; pin along folded edge. Turning raw edges under ½″ and mitering corners, stitch corners and stitch border edge to lining. Remove all basting threads.

NOTE *On Rainbow Block, black outline of butterfly is made of piping to give three-dimensional effect. If you wish to use piping in this manner, simply pin and sew piping in place with raw edges turned in, to be covered by wings. Appliqué wings in place over piping edges. If you prefer a flat surface for butterfly, cut and appliqué piece from black fabric, appliquéing wings on top.*

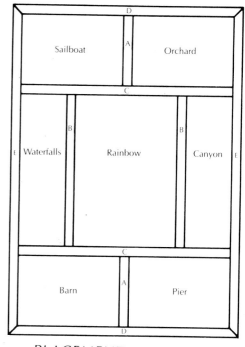

PLACEMENT DIAGRAM

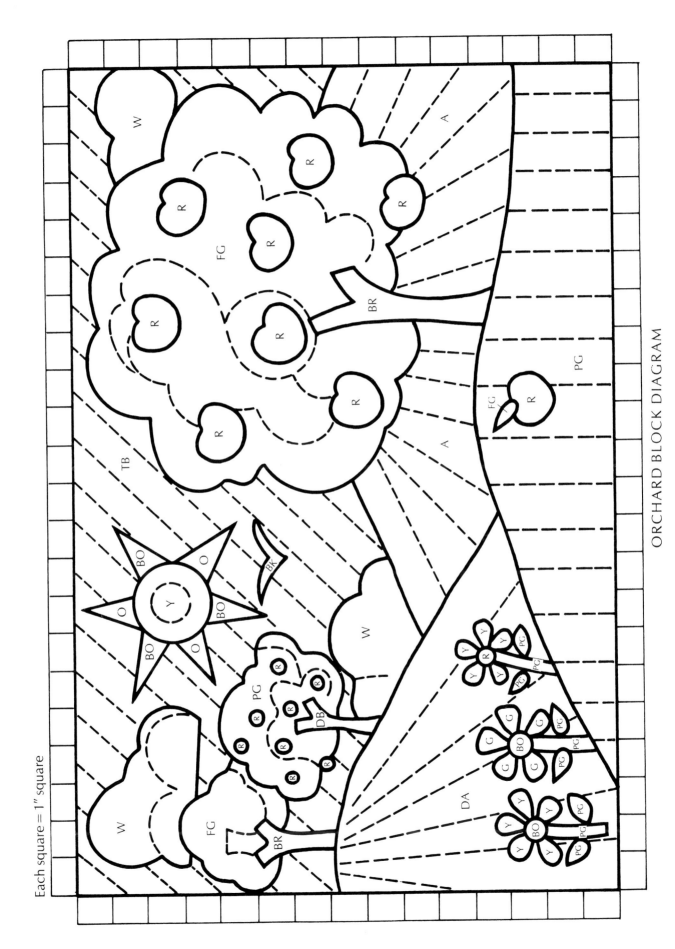

Each square = 1" square

ORCHARD BLOCK DIAGRAM

Each square = 1" square

BARN BLOCK DIAGRAM

Each square = 1" square

PIER BLOCK DIAGRAM

Each square = 1" square

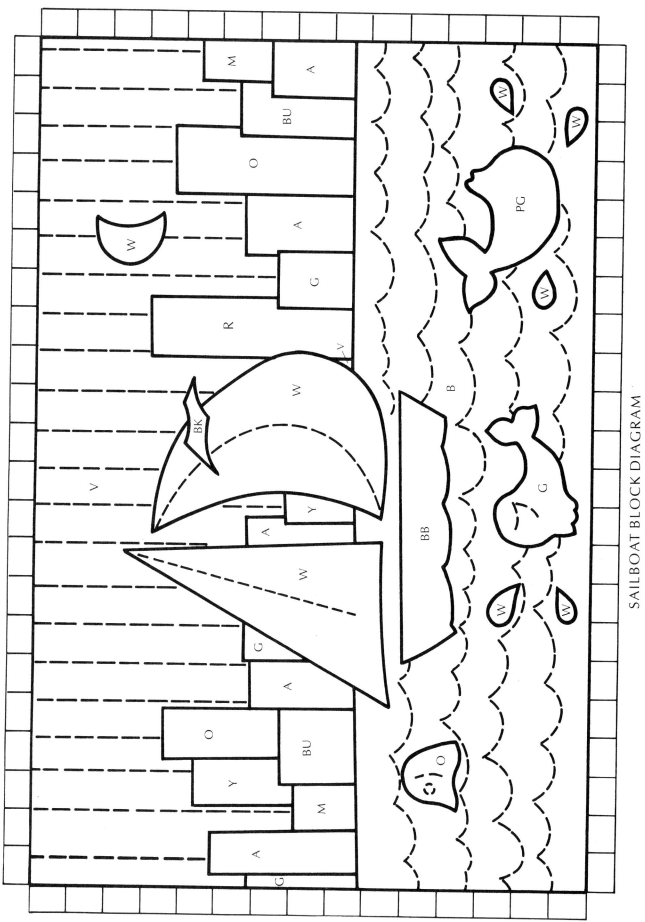

SAILBOAT BLOCK DIAGRAM

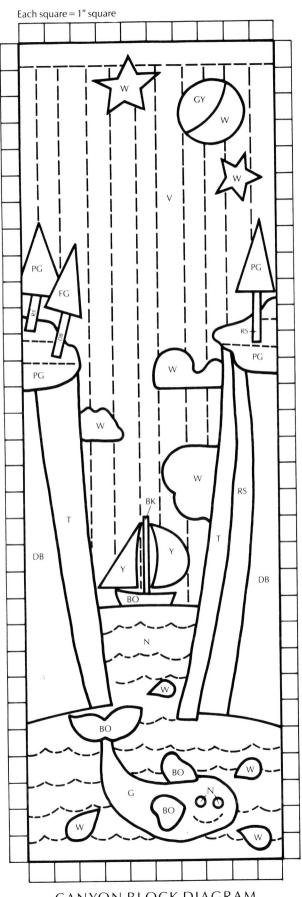

CANYON BLOCK DIAGRAM

Each square = 1" square

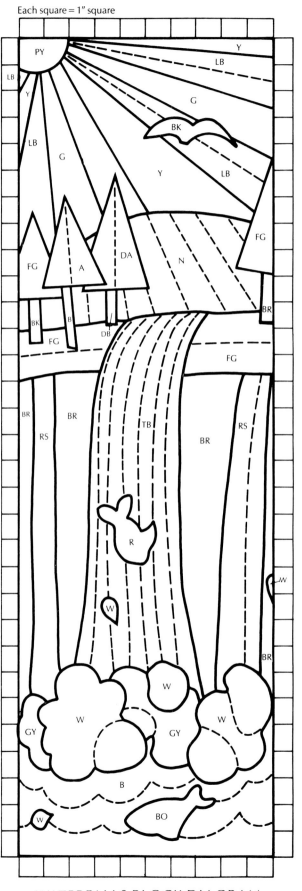

WATERFALLS BLOCK DIAGRAM

NORTHWEST INDIAN COVERLET

A bedspread by Juin Foresman of Laguna Niguel, California

Shapes in black, browns and beiges, cut from fabrics especially chosen for their homespun look and texture, combine in this bold, multi-layered appliqué coverlet, based upon traditional animal symbols of the Northwest Coastal Indian tribes.

about Juin Foresman

Juin Foresman's superb spread is truly a museum-quality work. Choosing fabrics with an earthy roughness and using characteristic Indian designs — specifically, the eye and tail of the killer whale and other configurations found on ancient Chilkat blankets or ceremonial robes — Juin executed the coverlet design in a layered appliqué technique. A raised, machine-sewn satin stitch outlines and emphasizes each facet of the design in a style typical of the original art forms. To carry the authenticity even further, the lower edge of the spread is V-shaped and fringed, as were the ceremonial blankets of the Northwest fishing tribes.

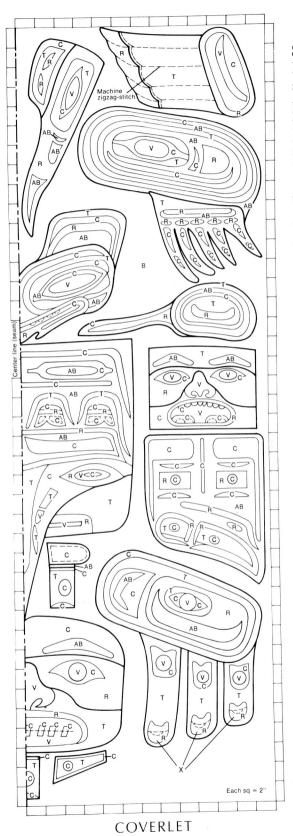

Machine zigzag-stitch

Center line (seam)

B

Each sq = 2"

X

COVERLET

SIZES Coverlet measures about 72" x 92", plus fringe at lower edge. Coordinating pillows: end pillows measure 18" square, center pillow measures 18" x 23".

MATERIALS 45"-wide black homespun-type fabric for background and some appliqués: 6½ yds. for coverlet, 2½ yds. for all 3 pillows; 45"-wide fabrics (lighter weight than background) for appliqués: 2 yds. each taupe and cream and 1 yd. rust for coverlet, ¾ yd. each taupe and cream and ½ yd. rust for pillows; also for appliqué, 45"-wide black velveteen or corduroy: 1 yd. for coverlet, ¼ yd. for pillows; black, rust, brown and tan sewing threads; about 550 yds. natural homespun yarn for coverlet fringe; polyester fiberfill and 2½ yds. muslin for pillows.

COVERLET: Background From black fabric, cut two 38" x 95" pieces. Stitch together along 95" edges to make ½"-deep center vertical seam. Topstitch 1" finished hems on all edges.

Appliqué Referring first to photograph for a visual impression of the coverlet, enlarge patterns (see How to Enlarge Patterns, page 255). Heavy lines indicate base appliqué piece for each unit; light lines indicate smaller pieces that are layered and appliquéd on top of base piece; broken lines indicate machine embroidery details. Do not add seam allowances.

Following color key, cut pieces from fabrics. Cut two of each freestanding piece, and cut each of those at center line double — these shapes are only *half* of the actual motif. To appliqué, referring to pattern and photograph for placement, work narrow machine satin stitch over raw edges as follows: Using contrasting-color threads, appliqué smaller pieces in layers to each base piece to form unit before applying base piece to background. A few pieces, such as the rust pieces marked X at bottom of pattern, are worked in *reverse* appliqué. To do this, cut a hole in taupe piece the same shape but slightly smaller than rust piece. Then place rust behind opening in taupe and appliqué taupe edges. Work reverse appliqué on other small pieces, if desired.

Following broken lines, work machine satin stitch in desired colors for details.

Pin appliquéd units to background, centering the whole design and balancing corresponding motifs on the right and left sides. Machine-appliqué in place.

Fringe From background fabric, cut two 3" x 40" strips. Overlap ends and pin to form V-shape (see bottom of coverlet

in photograph). Miter pinned ends and stitch together. Turn in long edges ¼″ and press. Turn in ends to match edges of coverlet. Pin to background with center of V about 3″ below bottom center appliquéd unit. Cut yarn into yard lengths and twist together in groups of about 13 strands each. Fold groups in half and pin folded end of each group behind V strip, spreading out as shown. Topstitch all edges of V strip, catching yarn in stitching.

NOTE *Coverlet and pillows are composed of taupe, cream, rust and black pieces machine-appliquéd in narrow satin stitch to black background. Fringe is attached to lower edge of coverlet behind a narrow, V-shaped black appliquéd strip.*

Color Key
B Black background
   fabric
AB Appliqúe in black
    background fabric
T Taupe
C Cream
R Rust
V Velveteen (or corduroy),
   black

PILLOWS From both background fabric and muslin, cut two 19″ squares for each end pillow and two 19″ x 24″ pieces for center pillow. To make pillow forms, stitch corresponding muslin pieces together on 3 sides; turn, stuff and close openings.

Enlarge pillow patterns. For each pillow, cut out pieces, noting which are to be cut from folded fabric. Appliqué to center of a background piece in same manner as for coverlet, except for beak on center pillow. Broken lines on center pillow indicate placement of beak; follow beak pattern (which is slightly larger than placement outline to allow for padding) for beak itself. Appliqué smaller pieces to beak. For backing on beak extension, cut a piece of cream, extending from broken line to lower point. Satin-stitch backing to extension to form pocket with opening at broken line. Stuff pocket. Matching top edge of beak to Z line on pillow top, appliqué upper part of beak in place, padding as you go.

For each pillow, with right sides facing, stitch back to front, leaving 12″ opening. Turn, insert muslin pillow and close opening.

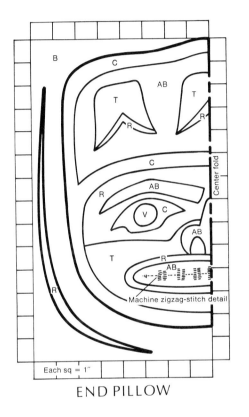

END PILLOW

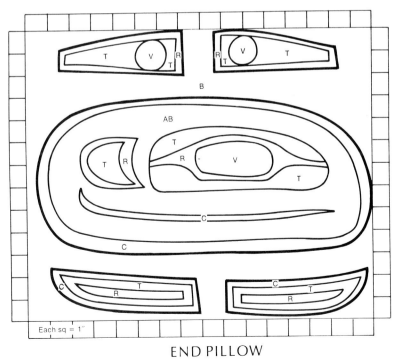

END PILLOW

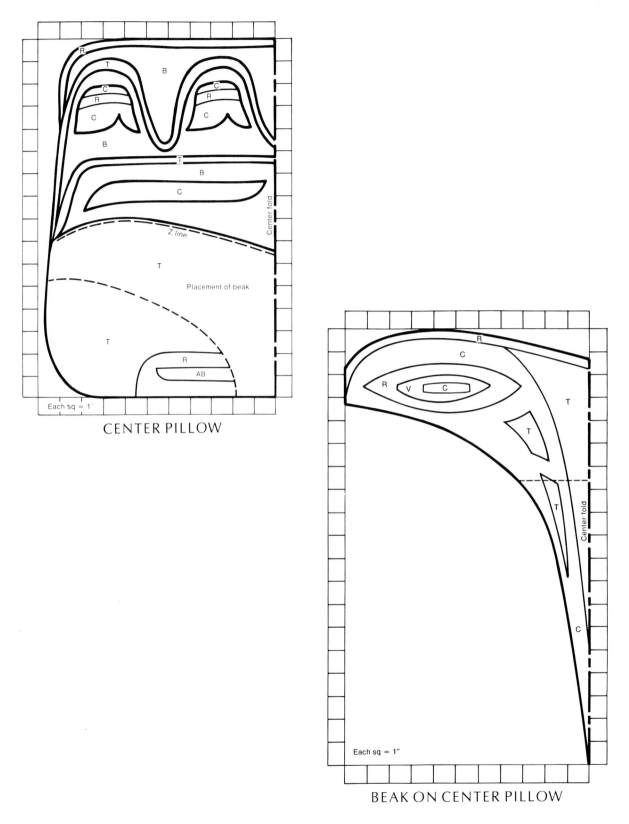

CENTER PILLOW

BEAK ON CENTER PILLOW

BUTTERFLY QUILT

An appliquéd and embroidered quilt by Mertie Caldwell of Tacoma, Washington

A combination of techniques — appliqué, straight sewing and embroidery — give an elusive, flower-fresh quality to this garden of delights.

about
Mertie Caldwell

Describing herself as "a senior citizen who has been quilting as long as I can remember," Mertie Caldwell is part of a family who believes in passing skills down from generation to generation. One of twelve children, she learned how to sew from her mother, and she picked up various other special techniques at many of the quilting bees so popular in Arkansas, where she grew up. For her butterfly quilt, she cut shapes from interfacing, and then ironed them onto her quilt fabric. She found that this makes the shapes easier to work with and keeps the fabric from ravelling as it is appliquéd. During quilting, the interfacing also helps to keep the patterns "puffy." Everything was sewn by hand — between Mertie's church activities and gardening chores.

SIZE About 76″ x 84″, finished.

MATERIALS One ½″-thick 81″ x 96″ polyester quilt batt; 45″-wide cotton-blend fabrics: 5 yds. white (or unbleached muslin) for block background, separating bands and binding, 4½ yds. print for lining, ¾ yd. print for border, 2 yds. total of assorted prints for butterflies, ½ yd. total of assorted scraps of solid colors for flowers, assorted solid greens for petals; ⅜ yd. 45″-wide black velveteen for large butterfly bodies; 6-strand embroidery floss (9-yd. skeins): about 50 skeins assorted colors, 12 skeins assorted shades of green and 10 skeins black; white sewing and quilting threads; quilting frame (available at Sears or craft stores).

APPLIQUÉD BLOCK From white fabric, cut an 18½″ square for background. Enlarge patterns (see How to Enlarge Patterns, page 255). Do not add seam allowance. Cut 4 pairs of large butterfly wings from different prints. Cut 4 flowers in assorted solid colors and 12 green leaves in various shades. Cut 4 black butterfly bodies. Following photograph for placement and spacing, pin butterflies, flowers and leaves to white square, placing them at least ¾″ in from edges. Working with 3 strands of floss, appliqué each piece in blanket stitch, making stitches about ⅛″ apart and using black for butterfly bodies, assorted colors for wings and flowers, light green on dark green leaves and dark green on light green leaves. Embroider details as indicated on pattern. (For stitch diagrams and instructions, see pages 238-242.) Appliqué 11 more blocks.

Half block From white fabric, cut a 9¾″ x 17½″ background. Cut 2 pairs of large butterfly wings, 2 flowers, 6 leaves and 2 butterfly bodies. Appliqué to background, arranging pieces as for half a block. Make 3 more half blocks.

BANDS: Short bands From white fabric, cut nine 4″ x 18½″ bands. For each band, cut out 2 small butterflies, 1 flower and 2 leaves. Working as for blocks, appliqué flowers and leaves to center of a band, and a butterfly, at an angle, on each side of flower. Work embroidery as indicated. Appliqué each band in same manner. From white fabric, cut three 4″ x 9¾″ bands to separate the half blocks; appliqué and embroider 2 small butterflies on each.

With right sides facing, making ½″ seams (use same seam size throughout), stitch one long edge of a band to edge of a block. Stitch opposite edge of same band to 2nd block. Add another band, a block, a band and a block to form strip. Make 2 more of these strips. Make one strip with half blocks and matching bands.

NOTE *Quilt is composed of twelve 17½″-square blocks, four half blocks, separating bands and border. Each block is appliquéd and embroidered separately in blanket stitch, then blocks and bands are joined and borders added. Top, batt and lining are basted together and quilted; edges are bound.*

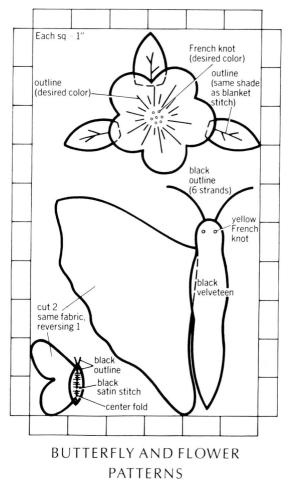

BUTTERFLY AND FLOWER
PATTERNS

Long bands From muslin, cut three 4"-wide bands the length of an assembled strip. For each band, cut out 12 small butterflies, 4 flowers and 8 leaves. Arrange them as desired along band (2 leaves per flower), pin in place, then appliqué and embroider. Stitch bands between strips to form quilt top.

BORDER From printed border fabric, cut two 3"-wide bands to fit length of quilt top, piecing as necessary for length. Stitch one border to each side edge. From same fabric, cut two more borders to fit top and bottom of quilt, including border width at each side. Stitch in place.

TO ASSEMBLE QUILT Cut and piece lining fabric to same size as top. Assemble top, batt and lining with batt centered in middle. Trim batt to about 1" larger all around than quilt. Baste layers together from top corners diagonally across to opposite lower corners, then across center from edge to edge in both directions.

TO QUILT Following directions that come with frame, mount quilt on frame. Working from center outward, quilt tiny running stitches through all layers. Quilt around each flower and butterfly just inside blanket stitches. Quilt 5 lines about ⅝" apart lengthwise along background on each separating band. Quilt diagonal lines about ½" apart along background on blocks. Starting ¼" from seam, quilt 4 lines ½" apart lengthwise along each border.

FINISHING Trim batt to same size as quilt lining. From white fabric, cut and piece 2½"-wide strips for binding to fit 2 side edges of quilt. With right sides together, making ½" seams, stitch to quilt edges; leaving ¾" of binding showing on right side, fold excess to wrong side, turn under seam allowance and stitch. Cut 2 strips each 1" longer than remaining 2 edges. Turn ends in ½" and bind quilt edges. Remove all basting threads.

ONCE-IN-A-LIFETIME COVERLET

An appliquéd coverlet by Laura Roos of Everett, Washington

An astonishing 16,500 pieces of fabric make this unusual creation a once-in-a-lifetime endeavor.

about Laura Roos

The crowning achievement of a woman who, in her own words, "was born with a thimble on my finger," Laura Roos' coverlet is based on an old sewing technique — a spectacular example of practicality going hand-in-hand with imagination and ingenuity. Using scraps of gingham, calico, percale and other cottons saved over the years, Laura sewed hundreds of small fabric squares into triangles and then appliquéd them, in concentric circles, onto muslin squares. To form blocks — forty-nine in all — outside corners are also filled in with the triangular shapes. Quilted borders are added all around, unifying a coverlet as sparkling and timeless as a precious jewel.

SIZE About 76″ square, finished.

MATERIALS 45″-wide cotton-blend fabrics: 3 yds. (turquoise used here) for borders, separating bands and some details, 4½ yds. of assorted solids and prints for blocks in *each* of following color ranges (see NOTE, right) — blues, reds, pinks, browns, greens, yellows and lavenders (31½ yds. in all); for corners on blocks, 3 shades of color used for bands and borders: ⅝ yd. of shade 1, 1⅛ yds. of shade 2 and 1½ yds. of shade 3; matching sewing threads; 6¾ yds. 45″-wide unbleached muslin for background on blocks and coverlet lining; cream-colored quilting thread.

BLOCK First select the fabrics you will use for one block, then cut 10½″ muslin square for background. Cut 1½″ square of fabric to use at center of block. Sew it out flat on exact center of background. Cut 6 more 1½″ squares from same fabric. Fold a square in half to form rectangle. Following diagrams for Block Triangle, establish center of folded edge and fold the 2 ends of rectangle to form a rough triangle with a neat point (raw edges at base will not be even); pin to hold. Fold each square in same manner and, with points meeting at center, form a circle of 6 triangles on center

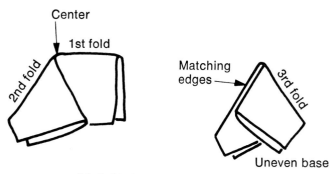

BLOCK TRIANGLE

BORDER TRIANGLE

NOTE *Coverlet is composed of 49 blocks each 9½″ square, finished. Each block top is made separately by folding small fabric squares into triangles and sewing them in 13 concentric circles to a muslin background, then adding corners. The colors were carefully chosen to follow coordinated color schemes. For example, in one block the circles are, from center out, light pink print, pink solid, dark pink print, medium pink print, light pink solid, pink-beige print, pink-white print, pink-green print, light pink solid, dark pink print, brown solid, pink-red print, light pink print. Other blocks might follow color schemes of yellow-brown-green or lavender-pink-purple or assorted blues. Corners are same on all blocks.*

Separating bands are appliquéd over edges of blocks and quilted, then borders and a row of triangles are added. Lining and top are assembled and lining is quilted.

square on background (sides of triangles will overlap a bit). Tack bases and sides of triangles to background, leaving points free. This is first circle of points. Make 10 triangles from 2nd fabric and tack around first circle in same manner with points about ⅜″ below points on first circle. Starting with 3rd circle, tack down point on each triangle as well as sides and base. Make 14 triangles for 3rd circle. Add 4 more triangles to each succeeding circle until 13 circles have been completed (54 triangles in 13th circle).

The corners of all blocks are alike and are made from 4 different shades of the color used for separating bands and borders. For each block, make 20 triangles from shade 3 (see Materials), 16 triangles from shade 2, 8 triangles from shade 1 and 4 triangles from same fabric as bands. To each corner tack 5 triangles of shade 3, 4 triangles of shade 2 and 2 triangles of shade 1. End with 1 remaining triangle on each corner to complete block. Trim triangles around edges even with muslin background; topstitch ¼″ from edge. Make 48 more blocks.

TO ASSEMBLE Lay out blocks in desired order, 7 blocks wide by 7 long. From fabrics for bands and borders, cut strips 1½″ wide, piecing if necessary, to make horizontal and vertical bands covering adjacent edges of blocks and for outer borders, making sure border strips overlap at corners of coverlet (16 strips in all — 12 bands and 4 borders). Turn long edges under ¼″ and press. Center the 12 bands over adjacent edges of blocks; pin, then slipstitch in place. Slipstitch borders around edge of coverlet, mitering corners. From same fabric, cut 36 pieces 1½″ square. Turn in edges ¼″ and press. Appliqué a square over each intersection of bands. Using matching sewing thread, quilt running stitches in a continuous X pattern along bands and borders (see photograph for pattern).

For border triangles, use any leftover border fabric and other prints and solids in same color range. For each triangle, cut a 1½″ square. Fold in half to form rectangle, then fold top corners at fold line to center as in Border Triangle diagram; press. Make enough triangles to fit around border. Slipstitch base of each triangle behind border.

Cut and piece muslin lining to same size as top (to points of triangles). Baste top and lining together (wrong sides facing) from top corners diagonally to opposite lower corners, then across center from edge to edge in both directions.

TO QUILT Spread coverlet out flat, lining side up. With pencil and ruler, lightly mark vertical lines about 6″ apart

across coverlet, then mark horizontal lines in same manner, dividing lining into squares. Starting from corners, mark diagonal lines, 6″ apart, in both directions, dividing each square into 4 triangles.

Coverlet can be mounted on a frame, lining side up, for quilting, but it is not necessary because these quilting stitches do not go through to right side of coverlet. You can work quilting, section by section, in your lap, simply by sewing small running stitches along pencil lines on lining and taking up just the background of blocks underneath. Quilt all lines with quilting thread.

Turn under muslin edges and slipstitch to backs of border triangles.

EMBROIDERED CRAZY QUILT

A pieced, appliquéd and embroidered quilt by Sarah S. Morgret of Romney, West Virginia

A crazy quilt to go mad about, this melange of velours, velvets, denims and corduroys worked every which way into fantasy shapes and playful images.

about
Sarah S. Morgret

As Sarah Morgret's quilt grew, so did her ideas for it, each element pointing her toward the next design to be worked. The freest of all free forms, the finished quilt was as much a surprise to her as to anyone else. "I was having so much fun," she explains, "that I knew I would love it no matter what it looked like." Sarah started with some embroidered jeans she had made a while before, cutting them up into patches and using these as the focal point for her twelve pattern blocks. She worked one square at a time, sewing down her denim patch, then dreaming up design elements in fabric and felt. These, after appliquéing, were embellished or joined with crewel embroidery.

NOTE *Full quilt is composed of twelve 23" square blocks, 2½"-wide separating bands and 1½"-wide borders. Each block is made separately (pieced, appliquéd and embroidered), then blocks are joined to bands. Top, batt or interfacing and lining are assembled and quilted or tufted, then finished with added border.*

SIZE About 82" x 107½", finished. Each block measures 23" square.

MATERIALS One ¼"-thick 90" x 108" polyester quilt batt (if desired for quilt use), *or* 6 yds. 45"-wide fabric for interfacing (if desired for wall hanging); 12 yds. 54"-wide navy fabric (wool or velour) for lining, separating bands, border and some patches for full quilt, *or* 1¼ yds. 54"-wide navy fabric for sample block wall hanging; scraps of textured fabrics such as corduroy, velveteen, wools, velour and blue jeans in shades of red (pinks to burgundy) and blues; scraps of felt in many colors, or in white, pinks, orange, yellow, brown and green for sample block; small amount of white knitting worsted for sample block; large-eyed needle for embroidery; sewing threads to match fabrics; dressmaker's carbon paper and tracing wheel.

Since the nature of any crazy quilt, and certainly this one, almost demands the freehand use of scraps, their placement determined by the color and random shape of individual fabric pieces, only one block has been selected for detailed directions. It is our hope that you will treat this block more as a guide and example than as a pattern to be copied exactly, using your own ideas about colors, materials, motifs and arrangement, and adding fanciful touches that you find personally pleasing. That way, your crazy quilt will be truly unique—and uniquely yours.

Directions are also included for finishing a single 23"-square block or the full quilt to be used as a wall hanging.

"INVENTING" YOUR OWN BLOCK This explanation is given first because the sample block directions, below, are so extensive that the shorter piece might get lost in the mass of details. Before attempting a block of your own, however, a reading of the sample block explanation is advised—many instructions will be clearer when you have an actual example in front of you.

Begin by planning the placement of your own choice of fabrics—for one block, enough to cover about a 24" square (the extra inch is for seam allowances around the edge). Cut scraps to desired shapes, adding ¼" seam allowance all around. With right sides together, stitch adjoining *straight* edges of shaped pieces together. Appliqué *curved* edges on pieces, first turning under and pressing seam allowance of piece to be appliquéd; clip seam allowance on curves. Pin piece in place and appliqué pressed edge, matching thread color to fabric. Join pieces to make a 24" square (includes ½" seam allowance all around).

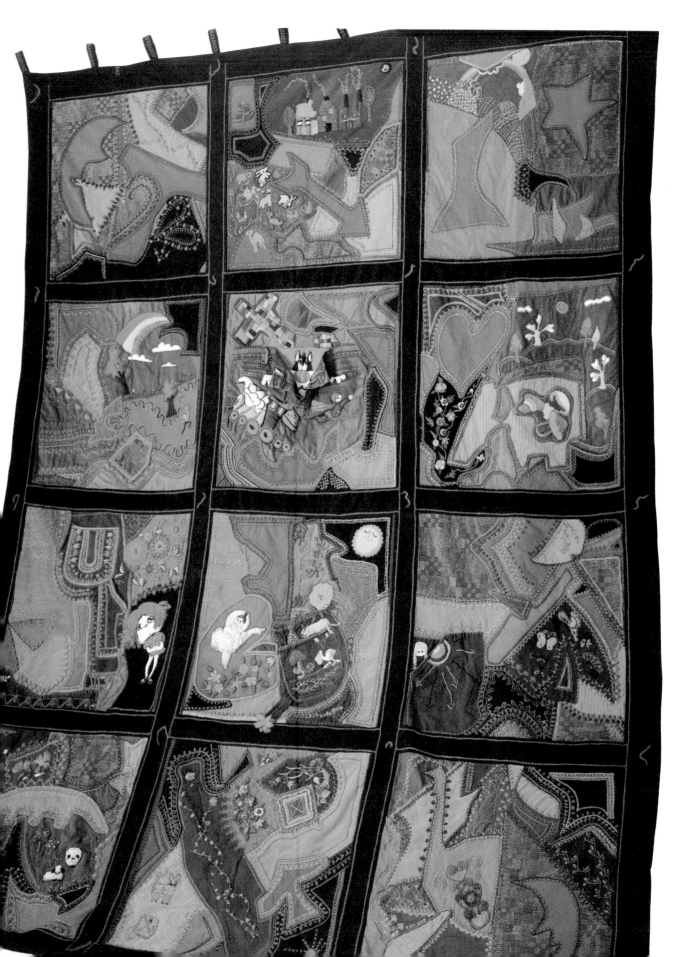

V	straight
⏀	lazy daisy
⋮	outline
‖	back or running
⪚	blanket
•	French knot
⧢	loop
⧤	chain
X	cross stitch
⑂	feather

Cut felt appliqué details as desired. Pin in position. Appliqué in place with embroidery stitches such as backstitch, outline stitch or blanket stitch. Appliqué pieces can be padded slightly with cotton for a three-dimensional effect. Embroider each color section of block in a style of your own choosing. See Embroidery Stitches, pages 238-242, for interesting stitches to use. Textured stitches, such as French knots, loop stitches, etc., can add richness to your work.

For full quilt or large wall hanging, make twelve different 24″ squares.

DETAILED SAMPLE BLOCK Enlarge patterns (see How to Enlarge Patterns, page 255), using heavy solid lines as pattern outline. Trace patterns on fabric, following color key below and leaving at least ½″ between pieces on fabric. Cut out pieces, adding ¼″ seam allowance all around. At outside edges of block, make ½″ seam allowances.

With right sides together, stitch adjoining straight edges of pieces together with ¼″ seams. Then appliqué the curved edges on each piece, turning under and pressing seam allowance of each piece to be appliquéd. Clip seam allowances on curves. Pin piece in place. Appliqué pressed edges, matching thread color to fabric. Firmly sew upper end of free-hanging ''tail'' (Section N) along pocket edge.

Decorate with felt appliqué and embroider each section, following Sample Block Diagram for placement, and detailed description below for colors. Separate 3-ply strands of crewel wool and embroider with single strand throughout unless otherwise indicated. See embroidery stitch key with diagram for stitches used (see Embroidery Stitches, pages 238-242, for working methods).

COLOR KEY BY SECTIONS

Section A *Fabric:* purple wool fabric with red and lilac stripes. *Border embroidery:* blanket stitch and outline stitch in hot pink.

Section B *Fabric:* Burgundy corduroy (arrows indicate direction of corduroy ribs). *Border embroidery:* Work from outside edge inward. Outline stitch in navy; flower straight stitches, outer V in royal blue, inner V in hot pink and center stitch in salmon; outline stitch in navy, running stitch in royal blue, backstitch in 2 strands of hot pink, running stitch in royal blue.

Section C *Fabric:* Cranberry red corduroy. *Border embroidery:* 3 outline stitch rows in salmon, royal blue and hot pink; running stitch in navy.

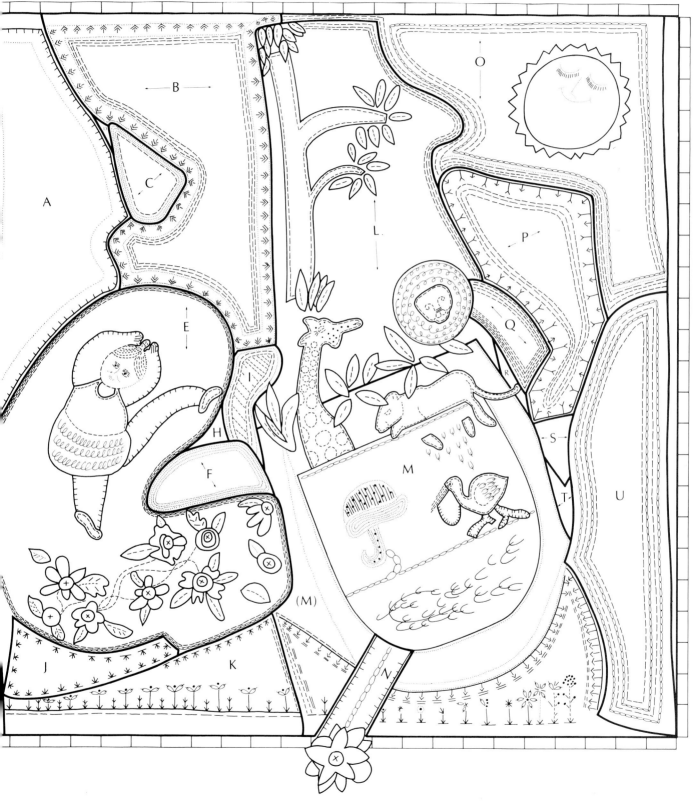

SAMPLE BLOCK DIAGRAM

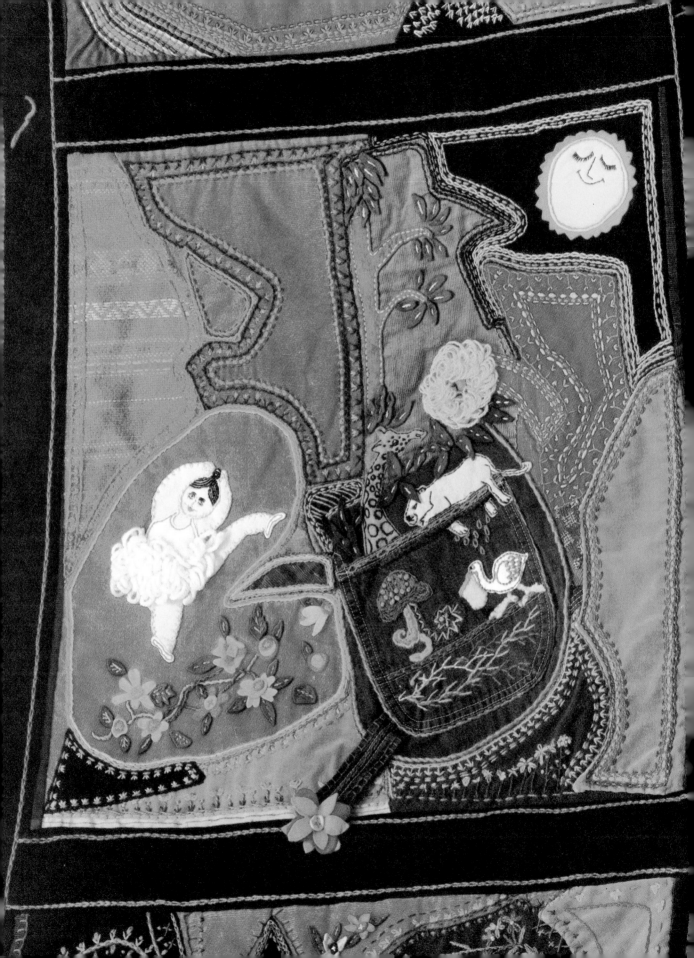

Section D *Fabric:* Cranberry red corduroy.

Section E *Fabric:* Cranberry red corduroy. *Felt appliqué details:* For ballerina, pale pink felt body with embroidery in pink blanket stitch and outline stitch, black outline stitch (hair and eyebrows), blue French dots (eyes) and rose lips; white felt tutu and slippers with embroidery in rose backstitch and loop stitch in white knitting worsted; for flowers, felt in various pink shades with some orange centers anchored with orange cross stitch, leaves in medium green with lime embroidery, stems in green and olive outline stitch. *Border embroidery:* Chain stitch in salmon, outline stitch in pink.

Section F *Fabric:* Wedgewood blue corduroy. *Border embroidery:* Four rows outline stitch in turquoise, pink, salmon and turquoise.

Section G *Fabric:* Royal blue corduroy.

Section H *Fabric:* Same as Section A.

Section I *Fabric:* Navy corduroy. *Border embroidery:* Outline stitch in hot pink, running stitch in pink, outline stitch in salmon. Diagonal outline stitch lines in hot pink.

Section J *Fabric:* Navy corduroy. *Border embroidery:* Straight stitches in hot pink; flower straight stitches, outer V in salmon, center stitch in pink.

Section K *Fabric:* Dusty rose velveteen. *Top border embroidery:* Straight stitch in turquoise; flower straight stitches, outer V in hot pink, inner stitch in salmon; straight stitch in turquoise. *Side border embroidery:* Two rows outline stitch in turquoise. *Bottom border embroidery:* Backstitch in 2 strands of hot pink, large blanket stitch in turquoise, leaf straight stitches in dark turquoise, large flower lazy daisy in salmon and French knot in hot pink; small flower straight stitches, outer V in hot pink, center stitch in salmon.

Section L *Fabric:* Light blue corduroy. *Felt appliqué details:* For tree trunk, brown felt with tan backstitch; leaves, green felt with lime embroidery. *Border embroidery:* Backstitch in 2 strands of navy, running stitch in green, backstitch in navy.

Section M *Fabric:* Scrap of blue jeans including hip pocket, or any blue fabric with a pocket patch hemmed at open top and appliquéd in place around curved edge. *Felt appliquéd details:* Orange felt giraffe embroidered in black; green felt leaves with lime embroidery; yellow felt lion with black embroidery; white felt pelican embroidered in turquoise with yellow pouch and feet embroidered with yellow, orange

embroidered beak. *Embroidered details:* Blue chain stitch across pocket top, green chain stitch across middle of pocket, blue lazy daisy stitches below lion; for mushroom, peacock top with magenta French knots; olive gills, magenta and purple stem with hot pink French knots, 2-strand hot pink chain stitches; overlapping feather stitches in brown, gold and yellow; 2-strand magenta outline around pocket; 3-strand magenta outline about 1″ beyond pocket edge. *Embroidery at bottom border:* Flower row, hot pink straight stitches, green stems and leaves, flower buds and tops in alternating shades of pink; remaining border, outline stitch in hot pink, blanket stitch in salmon, straight V stitches in pink, 2 rows of running stitch in hot pink and salmon.

Section N (free-hanging): *Fabric:* Blue denim. *Felt appliqué details:* Two flower shapes each of hot pink and orange felt and two yellow felt centers (1 pink and 1 orange flower, plus 1 yellow center, on each side of one end of the "tail"), tacked in place with orange cross stitch. *Embroidery:* Green chain stitch at center, green blanket stitch at each edge.

Section O *Fabric:* Navy corduroy. *Felt appliqué details:* Orange felt rays, yellow felt sun with orange backstitch and black face embroidery. *Embroidery around edge next to Section P:* Magenta backstitch, salmon outline stitch, hot pink backstitch, pink outline stitch. *Embroidery around edge next to Section L:* Two rows of backstitch in green and turquoise. *Border embroidery:* Gold chain stitch all around; then, on three sides only, orange running stitch, yellow backstitch.

Section P *Fabric:* Burgundy corduroy. *Border embroidery:* Hot pink blanket stitch (alternate long and short stitches); flower straight stitches, orange V on long stems, yellow inverted V on short stems; three rows of backstitch in yellow, magenta and yellow.

Section Q *Fabric:* Cranberry red corduroy. *Felt appliqué details:* Orange felt lion's face with black embroidery and gold loop stitch mane. *Border embroidery:* Five rows of running stitch in yellow, red, orange, hot pink and yellow.

Section R *Fabric:* Cranberry red corduroy.

Section S *Fabric:* Burgundy and blue print corduroy.

Section T *Fabric:* Light blue corduroy.

Section U *Fabric:* Dusty rose velveteen. *Border embroidery:* Turquoise chain stitch, 2-strand hot pink backstitch, red chain stitch, turquoise running stitch.

SINGLE BLOCK WALL HANGING: Assembling Cut 29″ square each from navy fabric for lining and from interfacing fabric, piecing if necessary. Assemble lining, interfacing (in middle) and block top centered on interfacing. Baste layers together from top corners diagonally across to opposite lower corners to keep layers from slipping.

Borders Cut four 7″ x 30″ border strips from navy fabric, piecing if necessary. With right sides together, making ½″ seams, center and stitch a border strip to each edge of block top, sewing to within last ½″ at each corner of block top (seamlines should meet at corners without crossing). Smooth border strips out to edge of lining, mitering corners; leaving 3″ border showing on right side, fold excess border fabric to wrong side over lining. Turning in ½″ raw edges and mitering corners, stitch corners and stitch border edge to lining. Embroider border with red chain stitches, if desired.

Hanging loops Cut four 2½″ x 8″ strips. With right sides together, fold strip lengthwise and seam 8″ edges together with ¼″ seams. Turn right side out and press flat with seam centered along underside of strip. Embroider strip, if desired. Fold strip in half crosswise to form loop. Position a loop at each end of top edge of wall hanging with other loops spaced equally between; fasten ends of each loop securely to underside of border.

FULL QUILT Make twelve 24″ squares. **To assemble top** From navy fabric, cut fifteen 3½″ x 24″ strips and four 3½″ x 105½″ strips for separating bands, piecing if necessary. Plan placement of blocks, arranging them 3 blocks across by 4 blocks long. With right sides together, making ½″ seams, stitch a 24″-long navy strip to top edge of each block; then join blocks in 3 vertical strips of 4 blocks each; join a 24″-long navy strip to bottom edge of each strip. Join vertical block strips and 4 long navy strips as follows: navy strip, then alternating vertical strips and navy strips. Embroider red chain stitch along separating bands ½″ from seam edges, if desired.

To assemble quilt Cut and piece navy fabric to make lining 82″ x 107½″. Cut optional interfacing (piecing as necessary) or quilt batt to same size. Assemble top, batt or interfacing if used, and lining with top centered on middle layer (if any) and lining. Baste layers together diagonally across top corners to opposite lower corners, then across center from edge to edge in both directions.

To quilt or tuft Original quilt, designed as a wall hanging, is not quilted. Instead, tufts are tied at each intersection of separating bands as follows: Thread 3-strand length of red crewel wool in needle. At an intersection of bands, on right side, insert needle through all layers, leaving 2″ end of wool on right side. Make a small stitch on wrong side, bringing needle back to right side. Cut yarn, leaving second 2″ end. Knot ends together securely. Repeat at each intersection.

If you plan to use quilt as a bed covering, you may wish to quilt fabrics for greater durability. To quilt, start at center and work outward, making inconspicuous running stitches through all layers, matching quilting or sewing threads to fabric being quilted and following outlines of sections and blocks.

Borders From navy fabric, cut two strips 4″ x 83″ and two strips 4″ x 108″, piecing strips if necessary. With right sides together, making ½″ seams, center and stitch an 83″-long strip to each narrow end and a 108″-long strip to each long side of quilt top, sewing to within last ½″ at each corner of quilt top (seamlines should meet at corners without crossing). Smooth border strips out to edge of lining, mitering corners; leaving 1½″ border showing on right side, fold excess border fabric to wrong side over lining; pin along folded edge. Turning in ½″ raw edges and mitering corners, stitch corners and stitch border edge to lining on underside. Embroider border with red chain stitches, if desired. Remove all basting threads.

Hanging loops for wall hanging Make and attach ten loops as for Single Block Wall Hanging.

COUNTED CROSS-STITCH

An embroidered coverlet by John Meren of Lexington, Ohio

Counted cross-stitch on open-weave cloth, a precise and painstaking technique, explodes with color in this star-upon-star design.

about John Meren

The counted cross-stitch designs seen years ago on a trip through Denmark continue to fascinate John Meren, and to motivate his own cross-stitch efforts. After ten years' experience with this technique, he was intrigued by the coverlet contest and began extensive research on old quilts, attending quilt shows and museum exhibitions. Partial credit for the star pattern he finally settled on is owed to the many variations he found among the quilt designs. Relatives and friends donated scraps of yarn, and John worked on his coverlet for a full year, "during every spare minute from my full-time job" as an accountant. He's enthusiastic about needlework and proud that he has "even convinced a few male friends to try their hand at cross-stitching."

SIZE About 76″ x 98″, finished.

MATERIALS 6 yds. 45″-wide even-weave cotton fabric with 5 counts per 1″ (see NOTE, right); 6 yds. 45″-wide fabric such as velveteen for lining; knitting worsted yarn, 4 ozs. each of navy, light blue, brown, dark green, yellow, burgundy and orange for panel colors, 2 ozs. each of pale green, mint green, olive, lilac, salmon, pink, rust, red, tan, mustard, gold, medium blue, aqua, rainbow ombré and small amounts of other assorted colors as desired for motif colors; tapestry needle; embroidery hoop.

GAUGE On fabric with 5 counts per inch, each motif measures about 5¼″ across; with fabric that has 5½ stitches per inch (see note), each motif measures about 4¾″ across. Cross-stitch embroidery is worked on even-weave fabric, that is, on fabric with the same number of threads woven across as are woven in length for each square inch. Cross-stitches are made by sewing over one thread in width and one thread in length.

On original coverlet, the even-weave fabric used has 5 counts per inch. If you have difficulty finding this exact fabric in your area, other even-weave fabrics can be used as background. You might, for instance, buy 5⅛ yds. of Pearl Aida, with 11 counts per inch, working stitches over two threads in each direction for a count of 5½ stitches per inch. (Coverlet will be smaller, about 70″ x 89″. More motifs and panels can be added to increase the finished size of the coverlet.)

TO PREPARE TOP Cut and piece even-weave fabric to make top 2″ larger on all sides than desired finished size. In piecing, take care to align meshes so weave remains even. Cover cut edges with masking tape to keep them from unraveling as you work.

EMBROIDERY Mark thread for first stitch at lower right corner 4″ in from the lower and right-side edges. For general stitch guidance, see cross-stitch, page 240, and backstitch, page 238.

Work in cross-stitch, making each stitch over one thread in each direction for 5-counts-per-1″ fabrics or over 2 threads in each direction on 11-counts-per-1″ fabrics, following chart as follows: Start at X and repeat from X to Y across, ending as at Z on last (12th) panel; start at R and repeat from R to S in length ending as at T on last (18th) motif. Work colors as follows (see photograph for guidance): In general, center portion of motif and backstitches (indicated by straight lines on chart) were worked in one color, remainder

NOTE *Coverlet is made by embroidering twelve panels of eighteen motifs each in cross-stitches worked by counting threads of background fabric. Embroidered top and lining are assembled and edges topstitched, with hanging tabs added if desired.*

of motif in contrasting color; motif border stitches and triangles below and above each motif in basic panel color and single vertical row of stitches between panels in a contrasting panel color. Colors used vary for each motif, but panel color remains the same for the length of an entire panel, except for fourth panel from right, on which panel colors vary at random (see photograph), to break the fixed pattern and add interest; similarly, on motifs, use ombré at random, or make a few motifs with 2 or more colors worked around center. Leaving 1 thread unworked, embroider a row of cross-stitches, in a panel color, horizontally across top and bottom edges of embroidered area.

Each square = one stitch

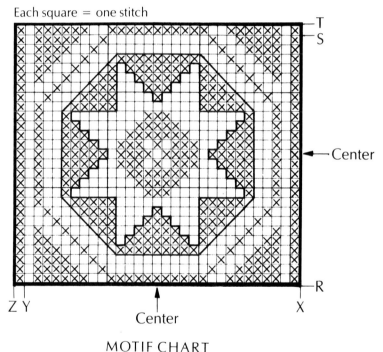

MOTIF CHART

☒ cross stitch

straight lines indicate backstitch

TO ASSEMBLE COVERLET When embroidery is completed, trim all around top to 2½″ from embroidered area. Cut and piece lining to same size as top.

Hanging tabs From lining fabric, cut five 2½″ x 6″ strips. Fold each strip in half lengthwise, with right sides together, and making ¼″ seams, stitch together along 6″ edges. Turn right side out and press with seam at center of underside.

Place top on lining, wrong sides together. Baste layers together from top corners diagonally across to lower corners.

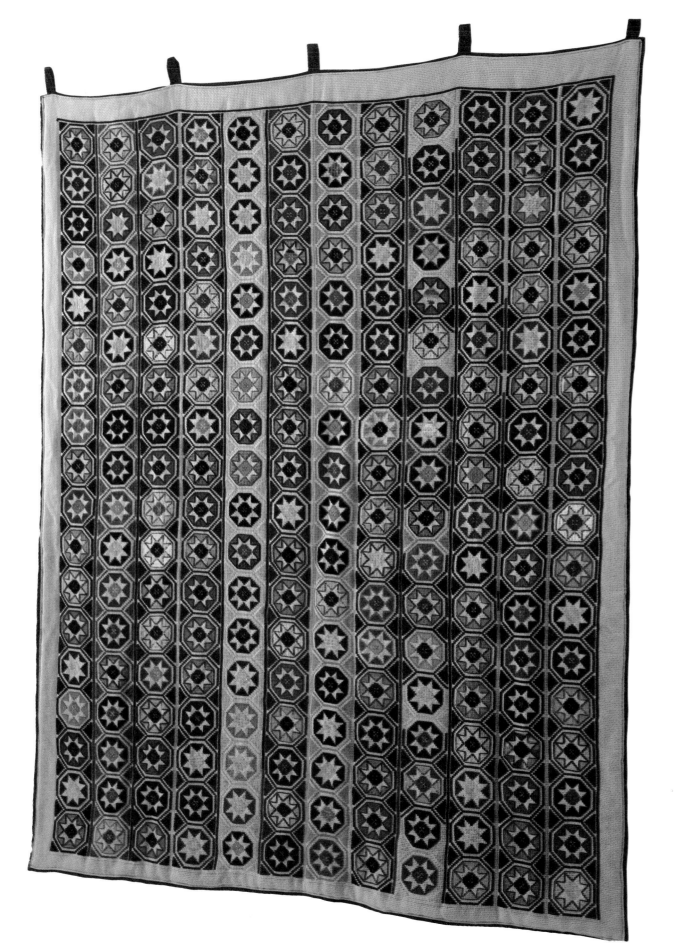

Turn in and press ½″ raw edges all around top and lining. Fold each tab in half crosswise to form loop and, spacing loops evenly along top edge, insert ends between turned edges of top and lining. Topstitch top and lining together all around, catching tab ends securely in stitching. Remove all basting threads.

PART 2 Crocheted Designs

For basic crochet instructions and reminders about techniques, see pages 242.

CROCHETED CIRCLES AND STARS

An afghan by Sara Griebel of Madison, New Jersey

Bright, bold colors in a geometric whirl make an afghan as powerful as a poster — and an easygoing, carry-along project in the bargain! Going around in the design, groups of granny-type circles joined with crocheted "stars."

about Sara Griebel

Sara Griebel picked her colors to complement the rug her husband was making; the bold pattern she designed for her afghan was improvised all the way. As Sara puts it, "The design was started in the center with the four gold circles joined in navy blue, surrounded with eight navy blue joined in red, surrounded by twelve navy blue to give a solid border. From then on it was trial and error until I reached the solid blue border surrounding the bright red. At that point I realized it was time to square it off. I finally decided to repeat part of the center motif for the corners — and completed it that way."

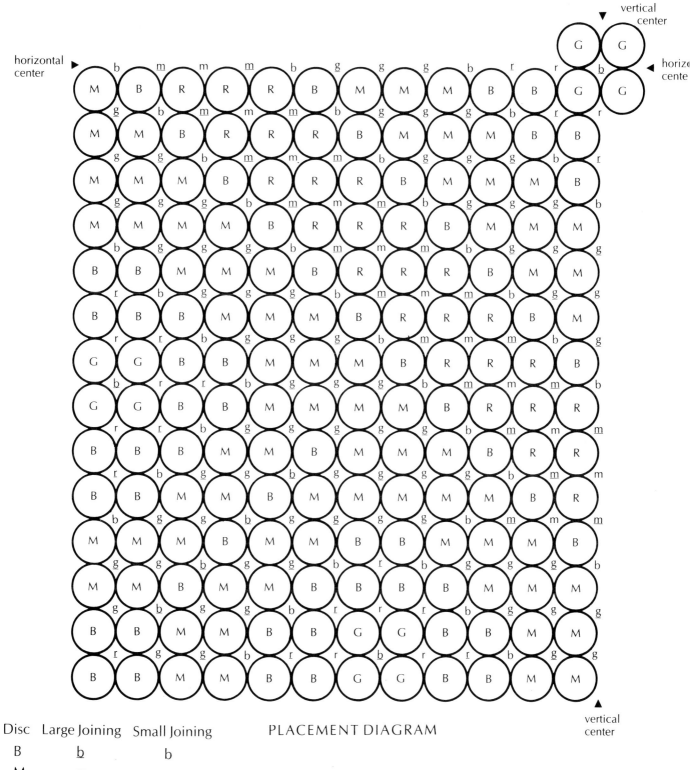

vertical center

horizontal center

horizontal center

vertical center

PLACEMENT DIAGRAM

Disc	Large Joining	Small Joining
B	b	b
M	m	m
R	r	r
G	g	g

SIZE About 75" x 106".

MATERIALS Knitting worsted: 36 ozs. royal blue (color B or b), 40 ozs. maroon (M or m), 20 ozs. red (R or r) and 24 ozs. gold (G or g); steel crochet hook No. O **or the size that will give you the correct gauge.**

GAUGE Disc measures 3" in diameter. On border, 11 sts (including ch) equal 2".

DISC Make 292 discs with color M, 236 with B, 108 with R and 36 with G. Ch 7. Join with sl st to form ring. **1st rnd** Work 14 sc over ring. Join with sl st to first sc. **2nd rnd** Ch 3, dc in first sc, work 2 dc in each remaining sc around (28 dc, counting ch-3 as first dc). **3rd rnd** Ch 4, skip ch-3, dc in next dc, * ch 1, dc in next dc. Repeat from * around. Break off.

TO ASSEMBLE Looking at Placement Diagram (page 136), find center of afghan where vertical and horizontal center lines cross. Beginning at center with 4 G discs, work Large Joining with color b as follows: **Large Joining** (see Large Joining Diagram): Ch 5. Join with sl st to form ring, ch 2, sc in top of a dc on first disc (position 1 on diagram), ch 2, sc over ring, ch 2, skip 1 dc on first disc, sc in next dc of disc (position 2), sc over ring, ch 5, skip 1 dc, sc in next dc (3), sc in dc of 2nd disc (4), ch 5, sc over ring, ch 2, continuing to skip 1 dc, sc in disc (5), ch 2, sc in disc (6), ch

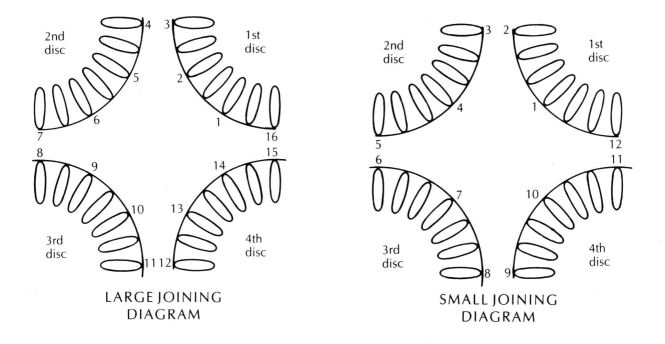

LARGE JOINING
DIAGRAM

SMALL JOINING
DIAGRAM

2, sc over ring, ch 5, sc in disc (7), sc in next disc (8), ch 5, sc over ring, ch 2, sc in disc (9), sc over ring, ch 2, sc in disc (10), ch 2, sc over ring, ch 5, sc in disc (11), sc in next disc (12), ch 5, sc over ring, ch 2, sc in disc (13), ch 2, sc over ring, ch 2, sc in disc (14), ch 2, sc over ring, ch 5, sc in disc (15), sc in first disc (16), ch 5, sc over ring. Sl st to ch-2. Break off.

Always having right side of work facing you, work from center out to assemble afghan, following Placement Diagram for disc colors (B, M, R and G) and type and color of joinings (b, m, r and g), working Large Joinings (indicated by *underlined* small letter) in same manner as before and working Small Joinings (indicated by *plain* small letter) as follows: **Small Joining** See Small Joining Diagram. Ch 5. Join with sl st to form ring. Ch 3, sc in dc of first disc (position 1 on diagram), ch 3, sc over ring, ch 5, skip 2 dc on first disc, sc in next dc (2), sc in dc of 2nd disc (3), ch 5, sc over ring, ch 3, continuing to skip 2 dc, sc in disc (4), ch 3, sc over ring, ch 5, sc in disc (5), sc in next disc (6), ch 5, sc over ring, ch 3, sc in disc (7), ch 3, sc over ring, ch 5, sc in disc (8), sc in next disc (9), ch 5, sc over ring, ch 3, sc in disc (10), ch 3, sc over ring, ch 5, sc in disc (11), sc in first disc (12), ch 5, sc over ring. Sl st to ch-3. Break off.

BORDER With right side of work facing you, attach R to a disc at edge. **1st rnd** Work sc in ch-1 sp between first 2 dc of edge disc, (ch 1, sc in next ch-1 sp) 9 times across each edge disc and for each corner disc, work sc in first ch-1 sp, (ch 1, sc in next ch-1 sp) 16 times. Border is slightly scalloped because of row following curve of disc and ''V'' formed where discs adjoin. **2nd rnd** With R, work (sc in next ch-1 sp, ch 1) around, but work sc between 2 sc at each V. **3rd rnd** With R, work (sc in next ch-1 sp, ch 1) around, but work 2 sc at each V, omitting the ch-1 between. Break off R; attach B. **4th rnd** With B, work same as for 2nd rnd. **5th rnd** With B, work (sc in next ch-1 sp, ch 1) around, but work hdc, ch 1 and hdc at each V. Border edge is now straighter. **6th rnd** With B, now work (sc in next ch-1 sp, ch 1) around, but work (sc in next ch-1 sp, ch 1, sc in same place, ch 1) once at each corner. **7th row** With B, work (sc in next ch-1 sp, ch 1) around. Break off.

OLD TIME MOVIE

*A crocheted afghan by
Martha Milligan of Dayton, Ohio*

*Here's a nostalgic "fragment" from
a reel of old film — Charlie
Chaplin's most beguiling expression, done in afghan stitch. Letters
are added to the finished piece and,
for a heightened illusion of vertical
motion, fringe "blurs" the edge as it
follows the colors of the film strip.*

*about
Martha Milligan*

Retired after twenty years' work in
public service, Martha Milligan enjoys her long-time hobbies of knitting and crocheting now more than
ever. She has created over twenty-
five afghans for friends and family,
confessing that she sometimes
spends "an entire day just on afghans because of the excitement of
seeing the finished product." Teaching herself crochet techniques over
the years and experiencing "lots of
ripping and other pitfalls," she is
proud of her skills and credits her
husband's talents as a commercial
artist for most of her designs, including this irresistible "Old Time
Movie."

NOTE *Afghan is crocheted in afghan stitch, using bobbins for large areas in black, white, pink and gray, with cross-stitch embroidery details and letters added in colors after afghan is crocheted, fringe added last. Pull balls can be used in place of bobbins; see page 255 for winding method.*

SIZE About 45" x 72", plus 4" fringe, as shown.

MATERIALS Knitting worsted: 18 ozs. each of black, natural-white and medium-gray, 2 ozs. each of medium gold, red, bright pink and emerald green; 14"-long aluminum afghan hook and aluminum crochet hook, both size J (or international size 6.00 mm) **or the size that will give you the correct gauge;** bobbins; tapestry needle.

GAUGE 4 sts = 1"; 7 rows = 2".

AFGHAN See instructions for working Afghan Stitch, page 248. With black and afghan hook, ch 175 to measure about 45". Now work across in afghan stitch of 175 lps (174 sts across — first lp is not a stitch), following Chart 1 for colors as follows: Using a bobbin or pull ball for each separate color area and following black lines only for crochet (red symbols indicate embroidery added later), work across entire chart, starting at A, working up from A to B, then C to B, then C to A in length (232 rows in all). With black only, sl st in each st across. Break off.

EMBROIDERY To work, see Cross-Stitch over Afghan Stitch, page 249. Following red symbols on Chart 1 and color key, embroider cross-stitches for details. Following Chart 2 for placement, embroider cross-stitch letters as indicated.

FINISHING With black and crochet hook, crochet a row of sc along each long (side) edge. **Fringe** To use as afghan, work a fringe, matching colors, in each stitch across top and bottom afghan edges as follows: Cut two 8" lengths of yarn; fold in half; with crochet hook, draw folded end from front to back through afghan stitch at edge. Pull cut ends through loop and draw tightly to secure. If you wish to hang your afghan, fringe bottom edge only. Finish top edge first with a row of sc, then a row of sl st to reinforce the edge.

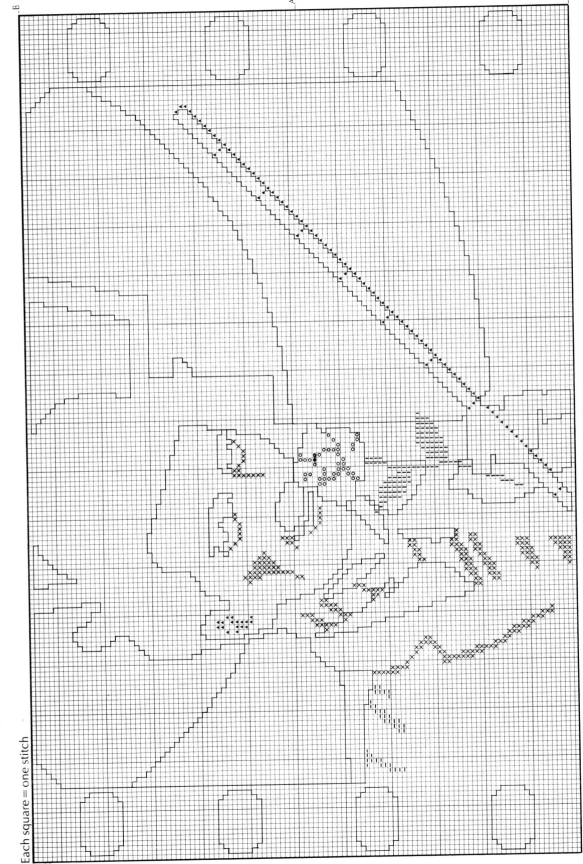

CHART 1

Color Key

Each square = one stitch

☐	crocheted background
⊙	red
⊠	gray
▲	black
⊓	green
⊟	white

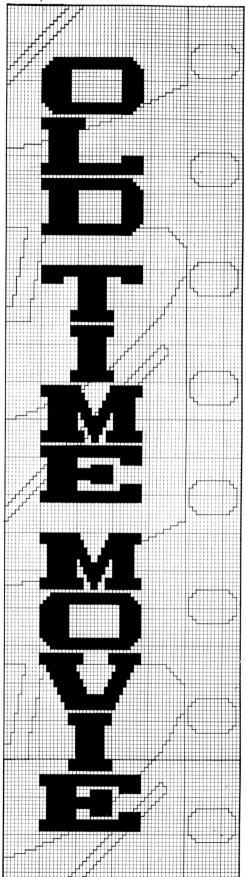

CHART 2

GRANNY VARIATION

A crocheted afghan by Eligene Buchanan of Santa Ana, California

Eight main pattern blocks — six done as granny squares and two in afghan stitch with cross-stitch embroidery — are repeated in a multitude of color variations and sewn together on the diagonal to make this dazzler of an afghan.

about Eligene Buchanan

Home decorating was what first started Eligene Buchanan toward her afghan. She wanted something to coordinate with the busy pattern of an upholstered chair in her bedroom — to give the impression that the chair "belonged." Concentrating on the eight main designs that appeared in the brushed velvet fabric, each set in a diamond shape, she went to work drafting her pattern ("ripping out and re-doing, crossing out notes and rewriting . . . until I was satisfied with the result"). She matched her yarn colors with those in the upholstery fabric and, with the confidence of someone who knows and loves crochet, she made all the blocks of one design before she drafted the pattern for the next.

SIZE About 50″ x 85″.

MATERIALS Knitting worsted: 16 ozs. gold (color G), 14 ozs. mustard (M), 8 ozs. each dark green (D), orange (O), light blue (B), white (W), light green (L) and pumpkin (P); aluminum afghan hook size J (or international hook size 6.00 mm); aluminum crochet hook size G (or international hook size 4.50 mm) **or the sizes that will give you the correct gauge;** large-eyed tapestry needle.

GAUGE With afghan hook, 4 sts = 1″; 4 rows = 1″. With crochet hook, 3 sts on average = 1″. Each square measures about 7½″ across.

SQUARE 1 (make 10): See instructions for Afghan Stitch, page 248. With afghan hook and color G, ch 28 to measure about 7″. Work in afghan st of 28 lps (27 sts — first lp is not a st) until 25 rows have been completed. Sl st in each st across. Break off.

Border With crochet hook and D, work 1 row sc evenly spaced around outer edge, working 3 sc in each corner sc; join. Break off.

Embroider cross-stitches on square, following Diagram 1. To work, see Cross-Stitch over Afghan Stitch, page 249.

SQUARE 2 (make 8): With afghan hook and M, ch 24 to measure about 6½″. Work in afghan st of 24 lps (23 sts) until 22 rows have been completed. Sl st in each st across. Break off.

Color Key

☐ background

☒ blue

☒ black

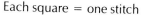
Each square = one stitch

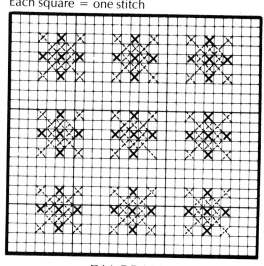

DIAGRAM 1

Border: 1st rnd With crochet hook and D, work sc evenly spaced around outer edge, working 3 sc in each corner sc; join. Break off. **2nd rnd** With G, dc in each sc around, working 3 dc in each corner sc; join. Break off.

Embroider cross-stitches in D and straight stitches in W on square, following Diagram 2.

SQUARE 3 (make 10): Starting at center with G, ch 6. Join with sl st to form ring. **1st rnd** Ch 3, work 2 dc in ring, ch 2, (3 dc in ring, ch 2) 3 times; join with sl st in top of ch-3. Break off. **2nd rnd** With O, * work (2 sc, ch 2 and 2 sc) in next sp, sc in next 3 sc. Repeat from * 3 times; join. Break off. **3rd rnd** With B, * work (2 tr, ch 2 and 2 tr) in next sp, skip next sc, tr in next 6 sc. Repeat from * 3 times; join. **4th rnd** Sk next tr, * work (2 sc, ch 2 and 2 sc) in next sp, sk next tr, sc in next tr, hdc in next tr, dc in next tr, (tr, ch 2 and tr) in next tr, dc in next tr, hdc in next tr, sc in next tr, sk next 2 tr. Repeat from * 3 times, omitting sk next tr on last repeat; join. Break off. **5th rnd** With W, * work (2 sc, ch 2 and 2 sc) in next ch-2 sp, skip next st, sc in next 4 sts, sk next st. Repeat from * 7 times more; join. Break off. Mark last ch-2 sp worked. **6th rnd** Starting in marked sp with G, * work (2 dc, ch 2 and 2 dc) in sp, sk next st, dc in next 5 sts, sc in next st, sk next st, sl st in next ch-2 sp, sk next st, sc in next st, dc in next 5 sts, sk next st. Repeat from * 3 times; join. **7th rnd** Ch 1, sc in next st, work (2 sc, ch 1 and 2 sc) in next sp, * sc in each st to next sp, work (2 sc, ch 1 and 2 sc) in next sp. Repeat from * twice more; sc in each st across; sl st in ch-1. Break off. **8th rnd** With B, * work 3 sc in next sp, sc in each sc to next sp. Repeat from * 3 times; join. Break off. **9th rnd** With O, * sl st in first sc of next corner 3-sc group, (ch 4, sk next sc, sl st in next 3 sc) 6 times. Repeat from * 3 times more; join. Break off. **10th rnd** With B, * work 3 sc in next corner sp, sk next sl st, dc in next 2 sl st, (sc in next sp, dc in next 3 sl st) 4 times, sc in next sp, dc in next 2 sl st, sk next sl st. Repeat from * 3 times; join. Break off.

SQUARE 4 (make 8): Starting at center with W, ch 6. Join with sl st to form ring. **1st rnd** Ch 1, work 8 sc in ring; join with sl st in ch-1. Break off. **2nd rnd** With O, * work (sc, ch 2 and sc) in next sc, sc in next sc. Repeat from * 3 times more; join. Break off. **3rd rnd** With G, * work (sc, ch 2 and sc) in next ch-2 sp, skip next sc, sc in next 2 sc. Repeat from * 3 times; join. Break off. **4th rnd** With D, * work (2 sc, ch 2 and 2 sc) in next ch-2 sp, (work long sc over next sc on 3rd row and into sc on 2nd row) 3 times. Repeat from * around; join. Break off. **5th rnd** With M, * sl st in next ch-2 sp, sl st

Each square = one stitch

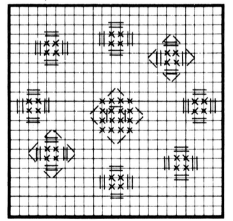

DIAGRAM 2

in next 2 sc, (ch 4, sl st in next sc) 4 times, sl st in next sc. Repeat from * 3 times; join. Break off. **6th rnd** With L, * working over sl sts of 5th rnd, sl st in next ch-2 sp on 4th row, ch 3, work cl as follows: (Yo, insert hook in same sp, yo and draw lp through, yo and draw through 2 lps on hook) twice, yo and draw through all 3 lps on hook (cl made), ch 3, sl st in same sp, (work 2 sc in next ch-4 lp) 4 times; join. Break off. **7th rnd** With G, ** work first triangle as follows: Sc in sp before next sc, * ch 6, sc in 2nd ch from hook, hdc in next ch, dc in next ch, tr in next 2 ch, sk next 4 sc, sc in sp before next sc. Repeat from * once to form 2nd triangle ending with sc in sp before cl, sl st in back of next cl. Repeat from ** 3 times; join. break off. **8th rnd** (**Note** This is not actually a rnd, but 4 separate ch lps.) *With W, sl st in top of 1st tr (2nd from base) of next triangle, ch 3, sl st in corresponding 2nd ch on adjacent side of next triangle. Break off. Repeat from * 3 times. **9th rnd** With O, * work sc in sp before next cl on 6th rnd, ch 1, sc in sp after cl, ch 2, sl st in back of next triangle on 7th row, ch 2, work (dc, ch 1, tr, ch 1, dc) in next ch-3 sp on 8th row, ch 2, sl st in back of next triangle, ch 2. Repeat from * 3 times; join. Break off. **10th rnd** With L, * work dc in first sc, dc in next ch-1 sp, dc in next sc, dc in next ch-2 sp, 2 sc in tip of triangle, dc in next ch-2 sp, dc in next dc, dc in next ch-1 sp, work (2 dc, ch 2, 2 dc) in next tr, dc in next ch-1 sp, dc in next dc, dc in next ch-2 sp, 2 sc in tip of next triangle, dc in next ch-2 sp. Repeat from * 3 times; join. **11th rnd** Ch 1, * sc in each st to next corner sp, work (2 sc, ch 2, 2 sc) in sp. Repeat from * 3 times, sc in each remaining st; join. Break off. **12th rnd** With G, sc in each sc around, working 3 sc in each corner ch-2 sp; join. Break off.

SQUARE 5 (make 8): Starting at center with P, ch 6. Join with sl st to form ring. **1st rnd** Ch 3, work 11 dc in ring; join with sl st in top of ch-3. Break off. **2nd rnd** With O, work 2 sc in sl st and in each dc around (24 sc); join. Break off. **3rd rnd** With W, * sl st in next sc, ch 4, work cl as follows: (Yo, insert hook in same sc, draw lp through and pull lp up to ½″) 3 times, yo and pull through all 7 lps on hook (cl made), ch 4, sl st in same sc, sl st in next 5 sc. Repeat from * 3 times; join. Break off. **4th rnd** With D, * work 2 dc in top of next cl, work 5 dc in next ch-4 sp, sk next sl st, (sc in next sl st, sk next sl st) 3 times, work 5 dc in next ch-4 sp. Repeat from * 3 times; join (4 petals formed). Break off. **5th rnd** With L, * sl st in center sc between next 2 petals, sk next sc, sc in next dc, hdc in next dc, 2 dc in next dc, 2 tr in next dc, 3 tr in

next dc, tr in next 2 dc, 3 tr in next dc, 2 tr in next dc, 2 dc in next dc, hdc in next dc, sc in next dc, sk next sc. Repeat from * 3 times; join. Break off. **6th rnd** With D, sk first sl st, sc, hdc, dc, make dtr in next dc as follows: Yo 3 times, insert hook in dc and pull lp through, (yo and pull through 2 lps) 4 times (dtr made); tr in next st, dc in next st, hdc in next st, sc in next 6 sts, hdc in next st, dc in next st, tr in next st, dtr in next st, * ch 6, sk next dc, hdc, sc, sl st, sc, hdc, dc, dtr in next st, tr in next st, dc in next st, hdc in next st, sc in next 6 sts, hdc in next st, dc in next st, tr in next st, dtr in next st. Repeat from * twice more, sl st in first dtr. Break off. **7th rnd** With O, * work (3 dc, ch 3, 3 dc) in next ch-6 sp, dc in next st, hdc in next st, sc in next st, sl st in next 8 sts, sc in next st, hdc in next st, dc in next st. Repeat from * 3 times; sl st in first dc. **8th rnd** Ch 3, * dc in each st to next sp, work (3 dc, ch 1, 3 dc) in next sp. Repeat from * 3 times, dc in each remaining st; join. Break off.

With 1 strand each B and G, tie adjacent dtrs on 6th rnd tog, knotting on wrong side.

SQUARE 6 (make 10): Starting at center with B, ch 6. Join with sl st to form ring. **1st rnd** Ch 1, work 8 sc in ring; join with sl st in ch-1. Break off. **2nd rnd** With O, work 3 dc in each sc around (24 dc); join. Break off. **3rd rnd** With L, * dc in next dc, work (dc, ch 3, dc) in next dc. Repeat from * around; join. Break off. **4th rnd** With D, * work 2 sc in next ch-3 sp, sk next dc, sc in next dc, sk next dc. Repeat from * around; join. Break off. **5th rnd** With G, sk 1st 2 sc, * work long sc as follows: Working over sc of 4th rnd, sc into dc on 3rd rnd (long sc made), sc and dc in next sc, ch 3, dc and sc in next sc. Repeat from * around; join. Break off. **6th rnd** With L, * sc in next long sc, work 5 sc in next ch-3 sp. Repeat from * around; join. Break off. **7th rnd** With P, work sc in back lp only of 2nd, 3rd and 4th sc of next 5-sc group, sk last sc of 5-sc group, work dtr in sp before next sc as follows: Yo 3 times, insert hook in sp and draw lp through, (yo and draw through 2 lps) 4 times, work dtr in sp after next sc. Repeat from * around; join. Break off. **8th rnd** With D, starting in first sc of 3-sc group, * tr in next sc, work (2 dtr, ch 3, 2 dtr) in next sc, tr in next sc, dc in next 2 dtr, dc in next sc, ch 1, sk next sc, sc in next sc, sc in next 2 dtr, ch 1, sk next 2 sc, dc in next sc, dc in next 2 dtr. Repeat from * 3 times; sl st in first tr. **9th rnd** Ch 3, dc in next 2 sts, * work (3 dc, ch 1, 3 dc) in next ch-3 sp, dc in each st and ch-1 sp to next ch-3 sp. Repeat from * 3 times, dc in each remaining st and ch-1 sp; join. Break off.

SQUARE 7 (make 10): Starting at center with W, ch 6. Join with sl st to form ring. **1st rnd** Ch 1, work 8 sc in ring; sl st in ch-1. Break off. **2nd rnd** With D, * work (3 dc in next sc) 8 times (24 dc); join. Break off. **3rd rnd** With G, * work (2 tr, ch 2, 2 tr) in next dc, tr in next 5 dc. Repeat from * 3 times; join. Break off. **4th rnd** With L, * work (2 dc, ch 2, 2 dc) in next ch-2 sp, sk next tr, sc in next 8 tr. Repeat from * around; join. Break off. **5th rnd** With O, * work (2 dc, ch 2, 2 dc) in next ch-2 sp, sk next st, dc in next 11 sts. Repeat from * 3 times; join. Break off. **6th rnd** With D, * work (2 sc, ch 2, 2 sc) in next ch-2 sp, sk next st, sc in next 14 sts. Repeat from * 3 times; join. Break off. **7th rnd** With P, * work (2 sc, ch 2, 2 sc) in next ch-2 sp, sk next st, sc in next 17 sts. Repeat from * 3 times; join. Break off. **8th rnd** With W, ** work (sc, ch 3, dc, ch 3, sc) in next ch-2 sp, sk next st, sc in next 6 sc, * work (sc, ch 3, dc, ch 3, sc) in next sc, sc in next 6 sc. Repeat from * once, then repeat from ** 3 times more; join. Break off. **9th rnd** With G, ** work 2 sc in next ch-3 sp, ch 1, work 2 sc in next ch-3 sp, sk next 2 sc, work (long dc over next sc and into sc on 7th row) 5 times, * sc in next dc, sk next 2 sc, work (long dc over next sc and into sc on 7th row) 5 times. Repeat from * once, then repeat from ** 3 times more; join. Break off.

SQUARE 8 (make 8): Starting at center with G, ch 6. Join with sl st to form ring. **1st rnd** Ch 1, work 12 sc in ring; join with sl st in ch-1. Break off. **2nd rnd** With O, * work (sc, ch 2, sc) in next sc, sc in next 2 sc. Repeat from * 3 times; join. Break off. **3rd rnd** With B, * work (sc, ch 2, sc) in next ch-2 sp, sc in next 4 sc. Repeat from * 3 times; join. Break off. **4th rnd** With D, * work (2 dc, ch 2, 2 dc) in next ch-2 sp, sk next sc, dc in next 2 sc, work long sc over next sc and into sc on 2nd row, dc in next 2 sc. Repeat from * 3 times; join. Break off. **5th rnd** With L, * work (2 dc, ch 2, 2 dc) in next ch-2 sp, dc in next dc, sc in next dc, ch 3, sk next 2 dc, sl st in next long sc, ch 3, sk next 2 dc, sc in next dc, dc in next dc. Repeat from * 3 times; join. **6th rnd** Ch 3, * dc in next dc, work (2 dc, ch 2, 2 dc) in next ch-2 sp, dc in next 2 dc, sc in next dc, sk next sc, 2 sc in next ch-3 sp, sl st in next sl st, 2 sc in next ch-3 sp, sk next sc, sc in next dc, dc in next dc. Repeat from * 3 times, omitting last dc on 3rd repeat; sl st in top of ch-3. Break off. **7th rnd** With P, * work (sc, dc, ch 2, dc, sc) in next ch-2 sp, sc in next 3 dc, hdc in next dc, dc in next sc, sk next sc, dc in next sc, sk next sl st, dc in

next sc, sk next sc, dc in next sc, hdc in next dc, sc in next 3 dc. Repeat from * 3 times; join. Break off. **8th rnd** With M, * work (2 dc, ch 2, 2 dc) in next ch-2 sp, dc in each st to next sp. Repeat from * 3 times; join. Break off. **9th rnd** Repeat 8th rnd once.

FINISHING Following Diagram 3 for placement, sew squares together with matching yarns.

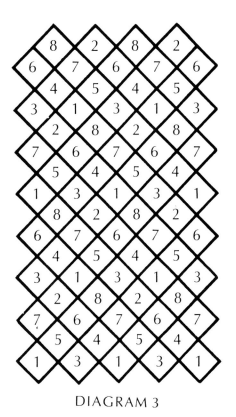

DIAGRAM 3

STAR OF BETHLEHEM, STAR OF DAVID

A crocheted afghan by Marjorie La Rue of Harvey, Illinois

Stark white crocheted stars, ablaze against a densely worked background, dominate this unusual two-color afghan. It is composed of eighty-four crocheted squares, repeats of four main motifs, arranged in a striking symmetrical pattern.

about Marjorie La Rue

An expert, and prolific, crocheter whose home is, in her own words, "furnished with my crochet," Marjorie La Rue responded to the stimulus of the contest by trying to think of a new design and technique. As she "meditated," she found her thoughts focusing on the religious symbol of a star, something she had never seen in an afghan. "It seemed appropriate," she explains, "that I use the stars of both faiths, Jewish and Christian, not only for contrast but also to show that Christians and Jews have a common bond." She chose the color blue because it is her favorite, but stars could not have a more compatible background.

SIZE About 46″ x 79″, finished.

MATERIALS Knitting worsted: 32 ozs. blue ombré, 16 ozs. royal blue and 16 ozs. white; aluminum crochet hook size H (or international size 5.00 mm) **or the size that will give you the correct gauge.**

GAUGE Each motif = 6¼″ square.

MOTIF 1 (make 24): **1st rnd** Starting at center with plain blue, ch 7, work dc in 7th ch from hook, ch 3, work (dc in same ch and ch 3) twice; sl st in 3rd ch of ch-6 (4 sp). **2nd rnd** Ch 3, work 2 dc, ch 1 and 3 dc in next sp, ch 1, * work 3 dc, ch 1 and 3 dc in next sp, ch 1. Repeat from * twice more. Join with sl st to top of ch-3. **3rd rnd** Sl st to next sp, ch 3, work 2 dc, ch 1 and 3 dc in next sp, ch 1, and 3 dc in next sp, ch 1, * work 3 dc, ch 1 and 3 dc in next sp, ch 1, work 3 dc in next sp, ch 1. Repeat from * twice more; join. **4th rnd** Sl st to next sp, ch 3, work 2 dc, ch 1 and 3 dc in next sp, ch 1, work (3 dc in next sp, ch 1) twice; * work 3 dc, ch 1 and 3 dc in next sp, ch 1, work (3 dc in next sp, ch 1) twice. Repeat from * twice more; join. Break off. **5th rnd** With ombré, * work 3 dc, ch 1 and 3 dc in next sp, ch 1, work (3 dc in next sp, ch 1) 3 times. Repeat from * 3 times more; join. Break off.

Star (make 24): With white, ch 2. **1st rnd** Work 5 sc in 2nd ch from hook; join. **2nd rnd** Ch 1, work 2 sc in each sc around (10 sc); join. **3rd rnd** (Ch 5, sl st in 2nd ch from hook, sc in next ch, hdc in next 2 ch, skip next sc, sl st in next sc; point made) 5 times; join. Break off. With white yarn, sew a star to center of each Motif 1.

MOTIF 2 (make 26): Starting at center with ombré, ch 4. Join with sl st to form ring. **1st rnd** Ch 3, work 2 dc in ring, ch 1, work (3 dc in ring, ch 1) 3 times. Join with sl st to top of ch-3. **2nd rnd** Sl st to next sp, ch 3, work 2 dc, ch 1 and 3 dc in next sp, ch 1, * work 3 dc, ch 1 and 3 dc in next sp, ch 1. Repeat from * twice more; join. **3rd and 4th rnds** Repeat 3rd and 4th rnds of Motif 1. **5th rnd** Sl st to next sp, ch 3, work 2 dc, ch 1 and 3 dc in next sp, ch 1, work (3 dc in next sp, ch 1) 3 times, * work 3 dc, ch 1 and 3 dc in next sp, ch 1, work (3 dc in next sp, ch 1) 3 times. Repeat from * twice more; join. Break off.

MOTIF 3 (make 17): Starting at center with blue, ch 4. Join with sl st to form ring. **1st rnd** Ch 3, dc in ring, ch 3, * (yo, insert hook in ring and draw up lp, yo and draw through first 2 lps on hook) twice, yo and draw through all 3 loops on hook, ch 3. Repeat from * 4 times more. Join with sl st to top of ch-3 (6 sp). Break off. **2nd rnd** With white, * work (5 dc

NOTE *Afghan is made of 84 crocheted squares with 4 different motifs, joined to form panel 7 squares by 12 squares and finished with a crocheted scalloped border.*

If desired, the afghan can be enlarged to make a bed-covering by adding more Motif 1 squares to center portion, surrounded by Motif 2 row and row of Motifs 3 and 4. Amounts of yarn given under Materials are for afghan only; if you make a larger-sized piece, be sure to purchase enough extra yarn.

in next sp) twice, work 6 dc in next sp. Repeat from * once more (32 dc). Sl st in first dc. Break off. **3rd rnd** With blue, * work 3 dc, ch 1 and 3 dc in next dc, skip next 3 dc, 3 dc in next dc, skip next 3 dc. Repeat from * 3 times more; join. Break off. **4th rnd** With ombré, * work 3 dc, ch 1 and 3 dc in next sp, ch 1, work (3 dc in next sp, ch 1) twice. Repeat from * 3 times more. Sl st in first dc. **5th rnd** Repeat 5th rnd of Motif 2.

MOTIF 4 (make 17): Work same as for Motif 3 with the following colors: 1 rnd each of white, blue, white and 2 rnds ombré.

FINISHING Following Placement Diagram, sew motifs together with ombré yarn. **Border** With right side facing you, using white, work scallop of sc, ch 3 and 2 dc in any sp; work scallop in each sp around, working 2 scallops at each corner and working scallop into adjacent sps at each joining as follows: sc in first sp, ch 3, work 2 dc in next sp. Join. Break off.

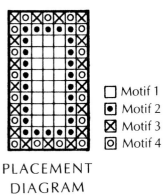

☐ Motif 1
⦿ Motif 2
☒ Motif 3
⊡ Motif 4

PLACEMENT
DIAGRAM

HIGHLAND THISTLE AND PLAID

A crocheted afghan by C. Beverly Manarin of Windsor, Ontario, Canada

Five strong plaid panels alternate with four soft-textured thistle panels, together evoking the colorings and designs of the Scottish Highlands.

about
C. Beverly Manarin

"Sometimes a certain stitch pattern presents an idea," comments Beverly Manarin, aptly describing how her beautiful afghan came about. She found that working single crochet into only one loop of every stitch produced a surface of loops that suggested to her a kind of huck embroidery ("the plaid evolved from this"). The surface was also perfect for her own "crochet appliqué" technique, in which floral patterns appear to be appliquéd but are actually attached by crochet "stems" right to the panel surface. This is how the thistles were created. Beverly feels that "the stem-crocheted method of attaching flowers and leaves eliminates the hours of sewing required for standard appliquéd designs" and recommends it for adapting floral design to crochet.

SIZE About 59″ x 61″, plus 5″ fringe.

MATERIALS Knitting worsted: 32 ozs. forest green (color F), 40 ozs. natural (N), 12 ozs. blue heather (B) and 4 ozs. each green heather (G) and kelly green (K); aluminum crochet hook size G (or international hook size 4:50 mm) **or the size that will give you the correct gauge;** large-eyed tapestry needle.

GAUGE 4 sc = 1″; 4 rows = 1″.

PLAID PANEL (make 5): With color F, ch 245 to measure about 61″. **1st row** (right side): Sc in 2nd ch from hook and in each ch across (244 sc). Ch 1, turn. **2nd row** Working in front lp only, sc in each sc across. Ch 1, turn. Repeating 2nd row for pattern st, work 3 more rows F, 1 N, 1 F, 1 G, 1 F, 1 N, 1 K, 8 B, 1 K, 1 N, 1 F, 1 G, 1 F, 1 N, and 5 F. Break off.

Starting at one end, with right side facing you, skip first 12 sts, * mark next st, (skip next st, mark next st) 8 times. Thread double strand F into tapestry needle. Starting at first marked st, weave strands under unworked lp of every other row across panel. Weave loosely enough to allow some give; be careful that yarn strands lie flat and untwisted. Fasten off. Repeat this process, starting at each of the next marked sts, in color sequence of 1 N, 1 K, 3 B, 1 K, 1 N and 1 F. Skip next 12 sts. Repeat from * 7 times.

THISTLE PANEL (make 4): With N, ch 245 to measure about 61″. **1st row** (wrong side): Sc in 2nd ch from hook and in each ch across (244 sc). Ch 1, turn. Repeating 2nd row of plaid panel, work until 18 rows have been completed. Break off. With right side facing you, using F, work 1 row sc across last row and across opposite side of starting chain.

STEM Mark row of unworked lps at center of panel. With F, work sc into each unworked lp, working lengthwise down panel.

Leaves (make 20): With F, ch 20. **1st row** Sl st in 2nd ch from hook, work (3 sc in next ch, sl st in next ch) 9 times. Break off, leaving 12″ end. Thread end in tapestry needle. Fold strip in half crosswise. Sew adjacent edges of starting chain together.

THISTLES (make 20) **Base** With F, ch 2. Work 6 sc in 2nd ch from hook; sl st in first sc. Break off, leaving 12″ end. Thread end in tapestry needle. Set work aside. **Flower** Wrap B around a 1½″-wide piece of cardboard 15 times. Insert separate strand B under wraps, slip wraps off cardboard, pull strand up tight and tie in knot. Bunch together at knot and insert in base. With tapestry needle and yarn end, sew edge of base around flower. Clip and trim flower to form tassel.

Following photograph, pin leaves and thistles to stem. Sew in place.

JOINING Join panels alternately, starting and ending with plaid panels as follows: With right sides together and working through both thicknesses with F, sl st adjacent sts together.

FRINGE Work fringe, evenly spaced, across each shorter end as follows: For each fringe, cut five 10″ lengths N. Holding lengths together, fold in half and, with crochet hook, draw folded end through edge from front to back, then draw ends through lp formed and pull up tight.

FLOWER FANTASY

A crocheted afghan by Sylvia Mater of San Bernardino, California

An unforgettable sight: A field of delicate flowers — daffodils, morning glories, daisies, roses, chrysanthemums, poppies and more, as realistic as can be in resplendent natural hues — abloom on an afghan that is the very picture of spring.

about Sylvia Mater

Sylvia Mater's story is one of courage and inspiration. A widow now badly afflicted with arthritis (only her hands are free from this painful handicap), she crochets her creations "for self-preservation" — to make a living by selling them, and to preserve her Czechoslovakian heritage and precious childhood memories. "I have to dream a lot," she writes. "My mother and grandmother were very close and as a little girl I went running with them through meadows, gentle slopes bedecked with flowers and watched over by giant trees. It was such a happy time . . . this inspired the 'Flower Fantasy'."

SIZE About 56″ x 72″.

MATERIALS Knitting worsted: *For background* 6 ozs. each violet, pumpkin, black and white; 4 ozs. hot pink; 3 ozs. each orange sherbet, coral, lavender, gold, pale rose and medium rose; 2 ozs. each turquoise, pale yellow, apple green, lime sherbet and natural. *For border* 13 ozs. green ombre, 6 ozs. apple green, 1 oz. each medium green and dark green. *For flowers and leaves* 13 ozs. assorted colors, plus leftovers from background and borders. *Other materials* Aluminum afghan hook size I (or international hook size 5.50 mm) and aluminum crochet hook size G (or international hook size 4.50 mm) **or the sizes that will give you the correct gauges;** sewing thread in appropriate colors for attaching flowers and leaves; tapestry needle, sewing needle.

GAUGES In afghan st with afghan hook, 9 sts = 2″; 3 rows = 1″. In sc with crochet hook, 9 sts = 2″; 5 rows = 1″.

BACKGROUND See instructions for Afghan Stitch, page 248. **Afghan strip** (make 7): Starting with first color at lower edge of diagram for each vertical strip and using afghan hook, ch 35 to measure about 7½″. Work in afghan st of 35 lps (34 sts—first lp is not a st), working 24 rows in each color until 8 squares have been completed on strip. Sl st in each st across. Break off. In this manner, make 7 vertical strips in all, following diagram and key for colors.

Sew strips together with matching yarn (matched to either of the adjoining colors), following diagram for placement.

BORDER 1st rnd With right side facing you, using crochet hook and green ombré, work sc, evenly spaced, around outer edge of background, working 3 sc at each corner; sl st in first sc. **2nd rnd** Ch 1, sc in each sc around, working 3 sc at each corner; sl st in ch-1. Break off.

Next row With right side facing you, working across sc of one narrow end only, with green ombré, sc in each sc across. Break off. Repeat this row 5 times more.

Work 6 rows in same manner across other end. Repeat 1st rnd around entire outer edge, then repeat 2nd rnd 3 times more. Break off.

Lace edging With right side facing you, with crochet hook, work across one narrow end as follows: **1st row** With medium green, sc in first 2 sc, * ch 4, skip about 1″ along edge (5 or 6 sc), sc in next 2 sc. Repeat from * 33 times more, ending last repeat in last 2 sc. Break off. **2nd row** Starting at beg of last row with apple green, sc in first 2 sc, ** ch 4; work cl as follows: Yo twice, insert hook in next sc

and draw lp through, (yo and draw through 2 lps) twice; * yo twice, insert hook in same sc and draw lp through, (yo and draw through 2 lps twice). Repeat from * once more, yo and draw through all 4 lps on hook (cl made); ch 3, work cl in next sc, ch 4, sc in next 2 sc. Repeat from ** across. Break off. **3rd row** Starting at beg of last row with apple green, dc in first 2 sc, * ch 5, work (cl, ch 3, cl) in next ch-3 sp, ch 5, dc in next 2 sc. Repeat from * across. Break off. **4th row** Starting at beg of last row with apple green, dc in first 2 dc, * ch 6, work (cl, ch 3, cl) in next ch-3 sp, ch 6, dc in next 2 dc. Repeat from * across. Break off. **5th row** Repeat 4th row, substituting ch 7 for ch 6. **6th row** Repeat 4th row, substituting ch 8 for ch 6. **7th row** Dc in first 2 dc, * ch 7, sc in top of next cl, work (dc, 3 tr, dc) in next ch-3 sp, sc in top of next ch, ch 7, dc in next 2 dc. Repeat from * across. Break off. **Last 2 rnds** ** With right side facing you, with crochet hook and ombré, work sc in each ombré sc along side edge. Break off ombré; attach apple green. Sc evenly spaced across edge of lace edging rows; work across 7th row as follows: Sc in first 2 dc, * ch 7, sc in next sc, dc, 3 tr, dc and sc, ch 7, sc in next 2 dc. Repeat from * across; sc evenly spaced across edge of lace edging rows. Break off apple green; attach ombré. Repeat from ** once more; join. Break off.

N	P	M	W	C	V	G
S	B	T	V	L	P	Y
H	W	O	P	A	B	L
R	V	G	B	H	W	C
Y	P	L	W	R	V	O
A	B	H	V	M	P	S
G	W	R	P	O	B	N
M	V	C	B	T	W	H

PLACEMENT DIAGRAM

Color Key
A apple green
B black
C coral
G gold
H hot pink
L lavender
M medium rose
N natural
O orange sherbet
P pumpkin
R pale rose
S lime sherbet
T turquoise
V violet
W white
Y pale yellow

FLOWERS AND LEAVES Following photograph for color and placement and using crochet hook, work flowers and leaves as follows:

Daffodil: Corona Starting at base, ch 5. Join with sl st to form ring. **1st rnd** Ch 1, work 9 sc in ring; join with sl st in ch-1. **2nd rnd** Ch 1, sc in each sc around; join. **3rd rnd** Repeat 2nd rnd. **4th rnd** (Ch 3, sl st in next sc) 9 times. Break off. **Petals** Starting at center with contrasting color, ch 5. Join with sl st to form ring. **1st rnd** Work 12 sc in ring; sl st in first sc. **2nd rnd** Ch 5 (foundation ch for petal); break off; (skip next sc, sl st in next sc; ch 5 — foundation ch for petal; break off) 5 times. **3rd rnd** (Sl st in next sc; working along first side of next foundation ch, sc in next 4 ch, 3 sc in next ch; working along opposite side of ch, sc in next 4 ch) 6 times (6 petals made); join. Break off. Sew corona to center of petals.

Morning glory: Corona Starting at base, ch 5. Join with sl st to form ring. **1st rnd** Ch 1, work 6 sc in ring; join. **2nd rnd** Ch 1, sc in each sc around, inc 3 sc evenly spaced (9 sc); join. **3rd rnd** Repeat 2nd rnd (12 sc). **4th rnd** (Ch 3, sl st in next sc) 12 times; join. Break off. **Pistil** With tapestry needle and contrasting color yarn, tack yarn at center of inside of corona, make knots in yarn 1″ from tack, then tack in same place (center of corona) 1″ from knots. Break off.

Daisy A Starting at center, ch 5. Join with sl st to form ring. **1st rnd** Ch 1, work 10 sc in ring; join. Break off. **2nd rnd** (petals): With contrasting color, (sl st in next sc, ch 7, sl st in 2nd ch from hook and in next 5 ch, sl st in same sc) 10 times. Break off.

Daisy B Work as for Daisy A through 1st rnd. Do not break off. **2nd rnd** (petals): (Ch 7, sc in 2nd ch from hook and in next 5 ch, skip next sc on 1st rnd, sl st in next sc) 5 times. Break off. With contrasting color, work 3 French knots in center.

Half daisy Work as for Daisy A until 5 petals have been completed. Break off.

Loop petal flower Starting at center, ch 5. Join with sl st to form ring. **1st rnd** Ch 1, work 8 sc in ring; join. Break off. **2nd row** (petals): With contrasting color, (sl st in next sc, ch 10, sl st in same sc) 8 times. Break off.

Small posy Starting at center, ch 3. Join with sl st to form ring. **1st rnd** Work 4 sc in ring. **2nd rnd** (Ch 3, sl st in next sc) 4 times. Break off. With contrasting color, work 3 French knots in center.

NOTE *For French knot diagram and instructions, see page 240.*

Medium posy Starting at center, ch 4. Join with sl st to form ring. **1st rnd** Work 6 sc in ring. **2nd rnd** (Ch 3, sl st in next sc) 6 times. Break off. With contrasting color, work 3 French knots in center.

Large posy Starting at center, ch 5. Join with sl st to form ring. **1st rnd** Work 8 sc in ring. **2nd rnd** (Ch 3, sl st in next sc) 8 times. Break off. With contrasting color, work 4 French knots in center.

Small rose Starting at center, ch 5. Join with sl st to form ring. **1st rnd** Work 8 sc in ring. **2nd rnd** (Ch 3, work 2 dc in next sc, ch 3, sl st in next sc) 4 times. Break off. With contrasting color, work 3 French knots in center.

Medium rose Starting at center, ch 6. Join with sl st to form ring. **1st rnd** Work 6 sc in ring. **2nd rnd** (Ch 4, work 3 tr in next sc, ch 4, sl st in same sc) 6 times. Break off. With contrasting color, work 4 French knots in center.

Curly chrysanthemum Starting at center, ch 5. Join with sl st to form ring. **1st rnd** Ch 1, work 8 sc in ring; join. Break off. **2nd rnd** With contrasting color, (sl st in next sc, ch 8, sc in 2nd ch from hook and in next 6 ch, sl st in same sc of first rnd) 8 times. Break off.

Double rose Starting at center, ch 3. Join with sl st to form ring. **1st rnd** Work 3 sc in ring. **2nd rnd** (upper petals): (Ch 3, work 2 dc in front lp only of next sc, ch 3, sl st in front lp only of same sc) 3 times. **3rd rnd** (lower petals): (Ch 3, work 2 dc in back lp only of next sc, ch 3, sl st in back lp only of same sc) 3 times. Break off.

Oriental poppy Starting at center, ch 4. Join with sl st to form ring. **1st rnd** Ch 1, work 4 sc in ring; join. **2nd rnd** Ch 1, sc in each sc around, inc 3 sc as evenly spaced as possible (7 sc); join. Break off. **3rd rnd** With 2nd color, sl st in front lp only of next sc, (ch 3, sl st in front lp only of next sc) 6 times, ch 3, sl st in 1st sl st. Break off. **4th rnd** With 3rd color, (sl st in back lp only of next sc, ch 4, work 3 tr in same lp, ch 4, sl st in same lp) 7 times. Break off.

Carnation Make a 4″ long ch. Work lp sc (see below) in 2nd ch from hook and in each ch across. Break off. Form chain into coil and sew in place. **To make lp sc** With yarn, make lp about 1″ long around first two fingers of left hand, insert hook in next st and draw a bit of lp through st; remove fingers from lp, yo and draw through both lps on hook to complete sc.

Small poppy Starting at center, ch 4. Join with sl st to form ring. **1st rnd** Ch 1, work 4 sc in ring; join. **2nd rnd** Ch 1,

work 2 sc in each sc round; join. Break off. **3rd rnd** With contrasting color, work 2 dc in each sc around; join. Break off. With contrasting color, work 4 French knots in center.

Rosebud Ch 2. **1st row** Work sc in 2nd ch from hook; turn. **2nd row** Ch 3, (yo, insert hook in sc and draw lp through, yo and draw through 2 lps on hook) twice, yo and draw through all 3 lps on hook (cl made), ch 3, sl st in turning ch. Break off.

Flower bud Ch 3. Join with sl st to form ring. **1st rnd** Work 4 sc in ring. **2nd rnd** With contrasting color, (ch 3, work 2 dc in next sc, ch 3, sl st in next sc) twice. Break off.

Large leaf Ch 8. Sc in 2nd ch from hook, dc in next 5 ch, sc in next ch. Break off. With contrasting color, work along opposite side of ch as follows: Sc in first ch, dc in next 5 ch, sc in next ch. Break off.

Medium leaf Ch 6. Sc in 2nd ch from hook, hdc in next 2 ch, sc in next ch, sl st in next ch. Break off.

Small leaf Ch. 4. Sc in 2nd ch from hook, sc in next ch, sl st in next ch. Break off.

Rounded leaf Ch 6. Hdc in 2nd ch from hook, dc in next 3 ch, hdc in next ch; working along opposite side of ch, hdc in first ch, dc in next 3 ch, hdc in next ch, sl st in top of turning ch. Break off.

Long leaf Ch 8. Sl st in 2nd ch from hook and in next ch, sc in next 5 ch. Break off.

Sew flowers and leaves in place with sewing thread. Couch strands of yarn with matching thread for stems.

BLUE MOON

A crocheted afghan by Mary Ellen Thompson of Roswell, New Mexico

A full moon hovers behind a galaxy of stars, aglitter in the night sky.

*about
Mary Ellen Thompson*

Crochet was the perfect pastime for Mary Ellen Thompson, pregnant with her first child at age 41. It perfectly filled the bill as "something new, sedentary and inexpensive," and she soon found herself unraveling lots of old knitting, holding the crochet hook like a knitting needle and, right from the start, creating designs that would be sought after by yarn companies and national magazines. That was thirteen hard-working years ago, so it comes as no surprise that this talented, self-taught crocheter was ready with her own innovative prize-winner. "The technique for 'Blue Moon' came from much experience — using two colors on each row (and working over the unused one), cutting each row (built-in fringe) and working only from the front side in order to follow my graph more easily."

SIZE About 38″ x 52″, plus fringe.

MATERIALS Knitting worsted: 28 ozs. royal blue, 20 ozs. white and 4 ozs. light blue; aluminum crochet hook size K (or international hook size 7.00 mm) **or the size that will give you the correct gauge.**

GAUGE 7 sc = 2″; 3 rows = 1″.

AFGHAN With royal blue, ch 141 to measure about 38″. **First row** Sc in 2nd ch from hook and in each remaining ch across (140 sc). Break off royal blue, leaving 3″ ends. With 3″ ends, attach royal blue and white to beg of first row. Work chart (p. 170) as follows: Starting with the first row of chart and working sts over yarn not in use, sc across, working from W to X twice. Break off royal blue and white, leaving 3″ ends; attach yarns to beg of previous row. Now continue to follow chart, working sc and repeating from W to X twice across and working up to Y in length. Mark center of last row. **Next row** On first half of row, work next row of chart from W to X across; on last half of row, work first row of chart from W to X across. Continue in this manner, working chart from W to X across and continuing up to Z in length for first half of row (right-hand side of afghan) and on last half of row (left-hand side of afghan) from W to X across and from W to Y in length twice more.

Break off yarns when chart is completed.

FINISHING Sl st all around with right side of work facing you. Securely knot fringe ends and trim them to 2½″.

NOTE *Work with right side of work facing you throughout, breaking off yarn at end of each row and attaching at beginning of each new row. Yarn ends extend at each end of row, automatically forming fringe along sides.*

When working colors, carry strand of color not in use along top edge of work, working stitches of other color over strand to enclose it within stitches.

To change colors, work last stitch of old color as follows: Draw up a loop, drop old color, with new color yarn over and draw through loops on hook to complete stitch.

To work light blue moon, do not carry light blue across entire afghan, but attach a separate bobbin or pull ball for light blue and second section of royal blue area. To wind pull ball, see page 255.

Each square = one stitch

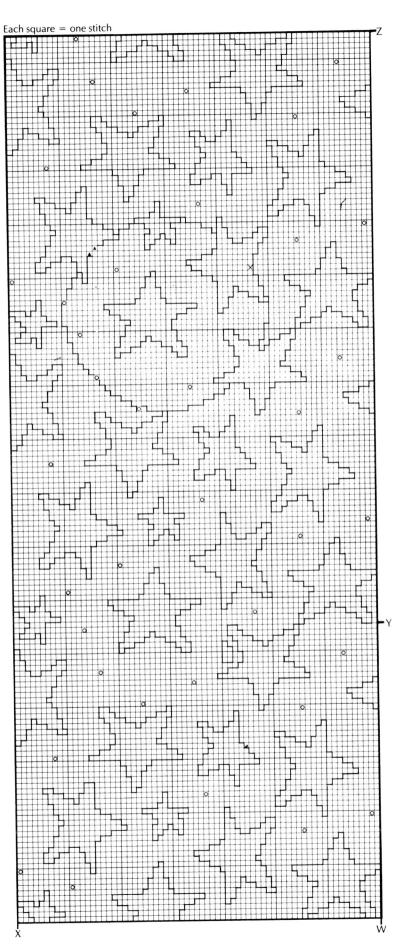

 background

☐ white

☒ light blue

▲ royal blue

NOTE *Background color is worked in royal blue, stars and single stitches (indicated by circle on chart) in white and moon in light blue.*

GRANDMOTHER'S FLOWER GARDEN

A crocheted afghan by Carol O'Barr of Knoxville, Tennessee

The clean geometric lines of a pieced coverlet — with hexagons, squares and triangles predominating — are adapted to crochet in this highly original, richly toned afghan. Everything is joined by crochet as the work progresses.

about Carol O'Barr

Carol O'Barr adores quilts but, she confesses, "being more of a crocheter at heart," she prefers to adapt traditional crochet motifs. About her contest entry, a tribute to her grandmother, she writes that "as lovely as the pattern is, it seemed to me that by itself it didn't look complete. This is why I chose to border the inset with half flowers, sawtooth and bear paw patterns," all derived from quilt motifs. Once she had laid out her afghan design, Carol crocheted it in a week, an astonishing feat for anyone — much less the mother of four children who admits to "burning the midnight oil many a night. But I didn't mind. I got so involved I just couldn't put it down."

SIZE About 40″ x 54″.

MATERIALS Knitting worsted: 12 ozs. cocoa (color A), 4 ozs. white (B), 6 ozs. beige (C), 4 ozs. pale blue (D), 2 ozs. each yellow-white ombré (J), pale pink (M), light blue (Q), green ombré (U), pale peach (V), 1 oz. each mint green (E), dark brown (F), medium brown (G), gold (H), rust (I), pale orange (K), orange-rust ombré (L), dark red (N), red-pink ombré (O), blue ombré (P), gray ombré (R), pale green (S), chartreuse (T); aluminum crochet hook size G (or international hook size 4:50 mm) **or the size that will give you the correct gauge.**

GAUGE Hexagon measures 2½″ across, measuring from corner to corner. Square measures 2½″ across.

AFGHAN Start by working center rectangular panel (see Afghan Diagram), composed of hexagons. Then add two side panels and two end panels. These sections are joined by an inner border and four corners of small squares, then a three-round outer border is added.

   To change colors Work with color in use until 2 lps of last st worked remain on hook; break off color in use; join new color; yo and draw lp through 2 lps on hook, then continue with new color.

WORKING PANELS Motif 1 (center): See Hexagon Diagram and Afghan Diagram. Starting at center with color D, ch 6. Join with sl st to form ring. Right side of work is always facing you. **1st rnd** Ch 5, work (dc in ring, ch 2) 5 times; sl st in 3rd ch of ch-5 (6 sp). **2nd rnd** * Work 2 sc, ch 3 and 2 sc in next sp. Repeat from * 5 times more. Join with sl st in first sc and break off. Put piece aside.

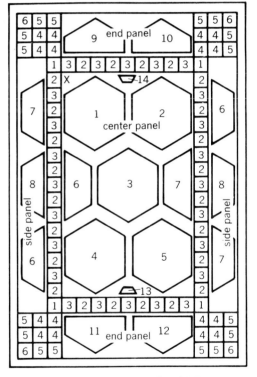

AFGHAN DIAGRAM

HEXAGON DIAGRAM

1st Ring With color P, make and join 6 more hexagons to center motif just completed as follows (see Hexagon Diagram): **1st Hexagon: 1st rnd** Work as for 1st rnd of center motif. **2nd rnd** Work 2 sc, ch 3 and 2 sc in first sp, in next sp work 2 sc and ch 1; pick up center motif and, holding wrong sides of both motifs together, sl st in any ch-3 sp on center motif, ch 1; then, working on new motif, work 2 sc in same sp as last 2 sc, work 2 sc in next sp, ch 1; then sl st in next ch-3 sp on center motif, ch 1; then, working on new motif, work 2 sc in same sp as last 2 sc; marking the first ch-3 worked, work 2 sc, ch 3 and 2 sc in each remaining sp on new motif; join and break off.

2nd Hexagon: 1st rnd Work as for center motif. **2nd rnd** Work 2 sc, ch 3 and 2 sc in first sp, in next sp work 2 sc and ch 1; pick up joined motifs just completed and, with wrong sides together, sl st in marked ch-3 sp, ch 1; then, working on new motif, work 2 sc in same sp as last 2 sc, in next sp work 2 sc and ch 1; then, working on joined motifs, sl st in same ch-3 sp on center motif that was used for previous joining, ch 1; working on new motif, work 2 sc in same sp as last 2 sc, in next sp work 2 sc and ch 1, join with sl st to next free ch-3 sp on center motif, ch 1; then, working on new motif, work 2 sc in same sp as last 2 sc; marking first ch-3 worked, work 2 sc, ch 3 and 2 sc in each remaining sp; join and break off.

Make and join 4 more motifs in same manner, but on last motif make 1 additional joining to first motif to complete ring. Mark last ch-3 on last motif worked.

2nd Ring With color Q, following Hexagon Diagram, work and join 12 more hexagons to joined motifs, joining first one in marked ch-3 sp. Put piece aside.

Working as for Motif 1, work Motif 2 (3, 4 and 5) using the following colors: For centers use H (K, C, E); for 1st Ring use I (L, R, T); for 2nd Ring use J (M, A, U).

Work partial-hexagon motifs in side and center panels with two center hexagons at base (marked with dots) in following colors, joining hexagons as shown within heavily outlined area on Hexagon Diagram:

Motif 6 (make 3): Center base N; outer 5 hexagons O.

Motif 7 (make 3): Center base F; outer 5 hexagons G.

Motif 8 (make 2): Center base L; outer 5 hexagons M.

Work half-hexagon motifs in end panels with center single half-hexagon (marked with circle) at base in following colors, joining hexagons and half-hexagons as shown within broken-line area outlined on Hexagon Diagram.

NOTE *Directions for single half-hexagon follow Motifs 9-12*

Motif 9 (make 1): Center half-hexagon S; 1st ring T; 2nd ring U.

Motif 10 (make 1): Center half-hexagon C; 1st ring R; 2nd ring A.

Motif 11 (make 1): Center half-hexagon H; 1st ring I; 2nd ring J.

Motif 12 (make 1): Center half-hexagon D; 1st ring P; 2nd ring Q.

Work **single half-hexagon** as follows: Ch 6. Join with sl st to form ring. **1st row** Ch 5, dc in ring, work (ch 2, dc in ring) 3 times (4 sp), ch 3, turn. **2nd row** In first sp work 2 sc; in next 2 sp work 2 sc, ch 3 and 2 sc; in last sp work 2 sc, ch 3 and sl st. Break off.

Half-hexagon Motif 13 (make 1): Work with O.

Half-hexagon Motif 14 (make 1): Work with G.

ASSEMBLY Following Afghan Diagram for placement of hexagon motifs, join motifs as follows with B, making single hexagons between motifs and filling in with half-hexagons on ends to make edges straight (see photograph):

1st rnd With B, form lp on hook. With right side facing you, work 3 dc, ch 5 and 3 dc in corner ch-3 sp at X on Afghan Diagram. ** Work along side edge as follows: * Ch 3, 3 sc in next ch-3 sp on hexagon, ch 3, 3 dc in next joining. Repeat from *, ending ch 3, 3 sc in next hexagon sp, ch 3, work 3 dc, ch 5 and 3 dc in corner ch-3 sp. Work along end as follows: * Ch 3, 3 dc in next joining, ch 3, 3 dc in center of next half-hexagon, ch 3, 3 dc in next joining. Repeat from * across, ending ch 3, work 3 dc, ch 5 and 3 dc in corner sp. Repeat from ** once more, ending ch 3, sl st in first dc. Break off. (There should be a total of twenty-nine 3-dc and 3-sc groups along each side of panel and seventeen 3-dc groups along each end of panel.)

2nd rnd With A, form lp on hook. With right side facing you, ** work 3 sc, ch 5 and 3 sc in any corner ch-5 sp, ch 3, * 3 sc in next sp, ch 3. Repeat from * to next corner sp. Repeat from ** around; sl st in first sc. Break off. (There should be thirty 3-sc groups along each side edge and eighteen 3-sc groups along each end.) Set aside.

SIDE PANELS Following Afghan Diagram for placement of hexagon motifs, join motifs as follows with C, making groups of 3 hexagons between motifs, 2 hexagons and 1 half-hexagon at each end (see photograph):

1st rnd With C, work in same manner as 1st rnd of center panel. (There should be a total of thirty-three 3-dc and 3-sc groups along each side and three 3-dc groups at each end—omit center of half-hexagon.) Set aside.

END PANELS Following Afghan Diagram for placement of hexagon motifs, use C and join motifs with groups of 4 whole and 3 half-hexagons between motifs, 1 hexagon and 1 half-hexagon at each end (see photograph). Set aside.

CENTER-PANEL BORDER: Solid-Color Square See colors below. Starting at center, ch 6. Join with sl st to form ring. **1st rnd** Ch 3, work 2 dc in ring, ch 2, work (3 dc in ring, ch 2) 3 times; join with sl st in top of ch-3. **2nd rnd** Sl st to next ch-2 sp, ch 3, work 2 dc, ch 2 and 3 dc in same sp, ch 2, * work 3 dc, ch 2 and 3 dc in next sp, ch 2. Repeat from * twice more; join. Break off.

Divided-Color Square See colors below. Starting at center with first color, ch 6. Join with sl st to form ring. **1st rnd** Ch 3; work 2 dc, ch 2 and 3 dc in ring, changing to 2nd color on last dc, ch 2; work (3 dc in ring, ch 2) twice; join with sl st in top of ch 3. Break off both colors. **2nd rnd** Make lp on hook with first color and sl st in sp before sl st on previous rnd; ch 3; work 2 dc in same sp; ch 2; work 3 dc, ch 2 and 3 dc in next sp; ch 2; work 3 dc in next sp, changing to 2nd color on last dc; ch 2; work 3 dc in same sp; ch 2; work 3 dc, ch 2 and 3 dc in next sp; ch 2; work 3 dc in next sp, ch 2; join. Break off both colors.

To join squares On 2nd rnd, work ch 1, sl st in adjacent sp on another square or on last rnd of appropriate panel.

Following Afghan Diagram and photograph for placement of squares, work and join each square to next square and to center panel as you go:

Square 1 D.
Square 2 C and D.
Square 3 D and V.

To join side panels With right side facing you, using A, work 2nd rnd around each side panel in same manner as 2nd rnd of center panel, substituting (ch 1, sl st in adjacent sp or joining on squares of center panel border, ch 1) for ch 3 along inner joining edge and (ch 2, sl st in adjacent ch-5 sp, ch 2) for ch 5 at each inner corner. (There should be thirty-four 3-sc groups at joining and outer edges and four 3-sc groups at each end.)

To join end panels Note that first and last square of center panel border is not joined. With right side facing you, with A, work as for 1st rnd of center panel, substituting sc's for all dc's on inner joining edge, and dc's for all sc's on outer edge, (ch 1, sl st in adjacent sp or joining on squares of center panel border, ch 1) for ch 3 along inner joining edge and (ch

2, sl st in adjacent ch-5 sp, ch 2) for ch 5 at each inner corner. (There should be eighteen 3-sc groups along joining edge, seventeen 3-dc groups along outer edge and six 3-dc and sc groups at each end.)

NINE-SQUARE CORNER SECTIONS Following Afghan Diagram and photograph for placement of squares, work and join each square to next square, to corner border squares and to edges of side and end panels as you go:

Square 4 A.

Square 5 A and C.

Square 6 C.

OUTER BORDER: 1st rnd With right side facing you, using A, ** work 3 dc, ch 5 and 3 dc in any corner sp, (ch 3, 3 dc in next sp, ch 3, 3 dc in next joining) 3 times, * ch 3, 3 dc in next sp. Repeat from * to next joining, ch 3, (3 dc in next joining, ch 3, 3 dc in next sp, ch 3) 3 times. Repeat from ** 3 times more; join with sl st in first dc. **2nd rnd** Sl st to next corner sp, ch 3, work 2 dc, ch 5 and 3 dc in corner sp, * ch 3, 3 dc in next sp. Repeat from * around, working 3 dc, ch 5 and 3 dc in each corner sp; join. **3rd rnd** Sl st to next corner sp, ** work sc, 5 dc and sc in corner sp, * work sc, 3 dc and sc in next sp. Repeat from * to next corner sp. Repeat from ** 3 times more; join. Break off.

PICTORIAL MEMORIES

*A crochet-appliqué coverlet by
Beatrice Barr Thompson of
Clinton, Arkansas*

The First Prize winner and an original in every sense, this collage of nostalgic "biographical" scenes features charming little crocheted figures appliquéd onto a flannel background. General instructions give tips for designing and depicting your own "life story."

*about
Beatrice Barr Thompson*

Plain-speaking Beatrice Barr Thompson (now close to 80) writes, "I learned to crochet when I was ten years old. My mother gave me a piece of grocery string and a crochet hook and taught me to make a chain. She told me when it was used up to unravel it and do it over and over 'til I wore it out. By that time, I didn't have to look at it to do it." That chain led to a lifelong interest in crochet, and in the creation of her "little people," as she calls the tiny figures she crochets. Beatrice assembled them into small, minutely remembered scenes from the events of a lifetime and couched them onto a blanket made from pieces of old flannel.

SIZE About 53″ x 69″, finished.

MATERIALS 4 yds. 36″-wide cotton or cotton-blend fabric in pink for lining; scraps of fabric or 2½ yds. 54″-wide gray flannel for background; small amounts of yarn (baby yarn, sport yarn and knitting worsted were all used on the original quilt) in assorted colors (on the original, pinks predominate, with pink ombré used for border motifs and trim); aluminum crochet hooks, size 00 for knitting worsted, size 4 for medium-weight yarns and size 9 for fine yarns.

GAUGE Gauge will vary with type of yarn used. Your work should be firm, but flexible enough, especially for arms and legs, that the work can be curved for realistic postures.

PLANNING CENTER PANEL Before starting, you may wish, first, to plan on graph paper a general placement of blocks within a rectangular center panel. Vary the block size as desired; small "leftover" spaces can be filled in with small motifs, a single figure, dates or your or others' initials. If total size of planned center panel differs from the dimensions of the original (about 45″ x 61″), be sure to make necessary adjustments in amounts of fabrics that must be purchased for background or lining. From gray flannel or other background fabric of your own choosing, cut out blocks, adding ½″ seam allowance all around.

Plan scenes for each block and make needed figures and details, following General Directions given below.

GENERAL DIRECTIONS FOR FIGURES Most of the crocheted figures were worked in medium-weight or fine yarns.

Adult woman with skirt With flesh-colored yarn, starting at top of head, make a chain ¾″ long. **1st row** Sc in 2nd ch from hook and in each remaining ch across. Ch 1, turn. Now work back and forth in sc until piece measures 1″ from beg. On next row, dec 1 st at beg and end of row (neck). Work 1 row even. **Next row** (arms and shoulders): Ch for 2″, sc in 2nd ch from hook and in each remaining ch, sc across neck sc; with separate strand of same yarn, make a 2″ chain and attach to last sc worked; with original yarn, sc in each ch of attached chain. Break off. Mark center ¾″ of last row for torso sts. Attach desired dress-color yarn to end st of marked torso sts. Ch 1, sc across torso sts. **NOTE** *If figure is not facing forward, skip next 2 rows.* **Next row** (bustline): Sc in first sc, work 4 dc in next sc, sc to last 2 sc, work 4 dc in next sc, sc in last sc. Ch 1, turn. **Next row** Sc in first sc, sc in first dc and last dc of next 4-dc group, sc to next 4-dc group, sc in

NOTE *Quilt was worked on 21 background blocks of various sizes, each depicting a scene or motif. Each block is worked separately, with crocheted figures and details sewn in place. Blocks are joined to form center panel; then strips of small blocks with crocheted motifs appliquéd are joined to form border around panel. Lining and binding trim are added.*

The scenes on the original quilt are ones from the designer's own life: children playing, ballet lessons, a bride, and so on. (See photograph.) Instead of exact directions for recreating the memories of the designer, general directions and suggestions are instead given for making figures, trees, flowers, small block motifs and border trim, so that you can make a similar quilt, but one that pictures your own special memories.

The designer made her quilt almost entirely from scraps she had on hand, purchasing only one skein of yarn for the project. Even the background fabric came from recycled coats.

It is hoped that you will feel free, too, to use your own scraps and yarn bits in colors that reflect your preferences.

first and last dc of group, sc in last sc. **NOTE** *For figures without bustline, inc 1 st at beg and end of next row.* Now work in sc until figure measures 1″ below neck. Dec 1 st at beg and end of next row (waist). Work 1 row even. Inc 1 st at beg and end of next row (hip shaping). Continue in sc, repeating inc row if needed to increase width of piece to 1¼″. Work until piece measures 1½″ below waist. Inc 1 st at beg and end of next row. Work even until piece measures 2″ below waist. Break off. For a more flared skirt, work more inc along edges below waist. For a still fuller skirt (see bridal gown) or ruffled skirt (see ballerina's tutu), work inc at edges and within rows (2 sc worked in 1 sc) as often as needed for desired fullness. Make a ¼″ chain at each edge of dress top for shoulder straps; tack in place.

For each leg, make a chain 1¾″. Sc in 2nd ch from hook and in each remaining ch. Break off. Attach shoe-color yarn (match to dress) to 2nd sc from one end of leg, work 5 sc around end of leg for shoe. Break off. Sew legs to underside of skirt bottom. For hair, attach desired color to edge of head. For simple bob or short haircut, crochet a row of sc around top of head. For curly hairdo, work several rows around and into first sc rows at top of head as follows: Work sc and ch 1 into each st around. Add more ch between sc for even curlier style. Add chains or braided strands of yarn for pigtails. Embroider eyes and mouths. When sewing figures to background, bend or curve arms and legs, tilt heads, etc., for more realistic poses.

Adult woman in trousers Work same as Woman with Skirt until piece measures 1″ below waist. Now work back and forth in sc across first half of sc only for 1½″. **Next row** (shoe): Sl st to center of row, ch 3, work 4 dc in center st. Break off. Attach yarn to last wide row on hip and work 2nd leg across 2nd half of row in same manner. When sewing figure to background, separate legs slightly. Add hair and face details as for Woman with Skirt.

Man or Boy No male figures appear on original quilt. However, Woman in Trousers figure can be adapted for a male figure, if desired. Make torso slightly larger for man or smaller for boy, and of course omit bustline.

Girl Work as for Woman until arms are completed. Mark center 1″ of last row for torso sts. Attach dress-color yarn to end torso st. Ch 1, sc across torso sts. On next row, inc 1 st at beg and end of row. Work 1 row even. Repeat these 2 rows until piece measures about 1½″ from beg of dress. Break off. Make ¼″ chain shoulder straps at top of dress; tack in place.

Make legs same as for Woman, omitting shoes, if desired. Work hair and face as for Woman.

Girl's dress can be varied with bottom ruffle as follows: Work until dress measures 1¼″ from beg. On next row, work 2 sc in each sc across. Work even in sc until dress measures 1½″ from beg.

Trees (trunks): Some thin trunks are crocheted chains of knitting worsted with a row of sl st worked across chain; these are sewn to background fabric with ridged side up and embroidered backstitch branches added. Thicker trunks are crocheted chains with a single row of sc worked across chain. The wide trunk was crocheted on a chain about 12″ long with rows of sc and shaping as follows: Crochet a chain of desired length. Mark position of curves. Work number of sc rows

required for desired thickness and at each marked curve on each row, inc to curve outward or dec to curve inward as needed. (The greater the inc or dec the sharper the curve.) Working in same manner, crochet and shape tree branches.

Leaves (individual leaves): With fine yarn, ch 5. Join with sl st to form ring. **Next row** * Ch 3, dc in ring, ch 3, sc in ring. Repeat from * 3 times more. Break off.

Chain of leaves Make foundation chain of desired length to fit all around tree top, starting at lowest branch, following under, then upper side of first branch, up trunk to next branch on same side of trunk, under and upper side of next branch, up trunk to next branch, and so on, working around and down to low branch of opposite side of trunk. **1st row** Spacing leaves along branches as desired, with a leaf worked at end of each branch, sl st in each of 3 ch, * make leaf as follows: Ch 3, sl st in same place as last sl st, ch 5, sl st in same place as last sl st, ch 3, sl st in same place, sl st in next 3 ch of foundation chain or to desired position for next leaf. Repeat from * along entire foundation chain. **NOTE** *Chain of leaves was also used for path borders.*

Flowers Work same as for individual leaves. **Other details** Fence posts, swings and outlines can be made with a chain of desired length with a row of sl st worked across chain. Chain can then be sewn to background in straight line or gently curved to desired outline.

ASSEMBLING BLOCK When you have crocheted desired pieces for an individual block, pin pieces in place. With matching sewing threads, neatly and securely tack pieces in place with tiny inconspicuous stitches. With yarn, add any embroidery touches you wish.

ASSEMBLING CENTER PANEL Arrange finished blocks to form rectangle, following your own plan for placement. With right sides together, stitch blocks together with ½″ seams to form center panel.

BORDER From gray flannel or other background fabric, cut enough 4½″ squares (measurement includes ½″ seam allowance all around) to fit all around center panel when joined (64 squares plus 2 filler rectangles used on original quilt).

Basic crocheted motif Motif measures about 2″ in diameter. With medium-weight ombré yarn, ch 5. Join with sl st to form ring. **1st rnd** Work 12 sc over ring. Join to first sc. **2nd rnd** Working in back loop only of each st around, * sc in next sc, ch 3, dc in next sc, ch 3, sc in next sc. Repeat from * 5 times more. Join to first sc. **3rd rnd** Working in back loop only, * ch 5, sl st in dc, ch 3, sl st in same dc (picot made), ch 5, sl st in next sc, skip next sc. Repeat from * around, ending with sl st in last sc. Break off.

Most motifs were crocheted this way. In a few cases, the motif was varied by making larger picot (ch 4 or 5 instead of ch 3), or the entire picot was eliminated by working an sc in top of dc (instead of sl sts and ch 3).

Also a few stars were made as follows: Complete 1st rnd as for Basic Motif. **2nd rnd** Working in back loop only, * sc in next sc, work 2 sc, ch 3 and 2 sc in next sc. Repeat from * 5 times more. Join to first sc. **3rd rnd** Working in back lp only, sc in first 2 sc, * skip next sc, over next ch-3 loop work 3 sc, ch 3 and 3 sc (point made), skip 1 sc, sc in next 3 sc. Repeat from * around, ending with sc in last sc. Break off.

Sew a motif to center of each square. With right sides together, making ½" seams, stitch squares together to form strip to fit top edge of center panel, adding a filler piece if necessary to make strip the exact length needed; stitch strip in place. In same manner, make strips of squares and sew in place at bottom edge and along sides. **NOTE** *Filler pieces are a good spot to embroider your initials or date.*

TO ASSEMBLE QUILT From pink cotton, cut lining 1" larger all around than assembled top, piecing fabric as necessary. Center assembled top, right side up, on top of lining. Baste layers together from top corners diagonally across to lower corners and across center from edge to edge in both directions. Machine-stitch layers together ½" in from edge of top. Fold excess lining fabric to *right* side of quilt, covering edges of top; miter corners. Turn under raw edges, forming ½" binding all around. Slipstitch binding in place.

BINDING TRIM With knitting worsted-weight ombré yarn, ch 5. **Next row** In 5th ch from hook, work dc and tr, * ch 4, work dc and tr in top of last tr. Repeat from * until trim is long enough to go all around quilt. Break off. Securely tack trim in place on narrow cotton binding.

TUFTING Original quilt is tufted, not quilted, to keep layers from slipping. To tuft, work as follows: For each tuft, cut two 1½" strands of yarn. Matching sewing thread to background color and working from wrong side, insert needle through layers, make a small stitch on right side, bringing needle through to wrong side. Make several more small stitches in same manner in same place, holding 1½" strands of yarn on wrong side and working stitches tightly over center of strands to form tuft. Fasten off sewing thread. Make tufts evenly spaced, about 15" apart, over entire quilt. Remove all basting threads.

NOTE *For embroidery diagrams and instructions, see pages 238-242.*

BLACK–AND–WHITE SPREAD

Crocheted cotton spread by Clara Neep of Sacramento, California

This graphic black-and-white bed-spread creates an unusual, optical art effect. The technique is unusual, too—contrasting threads dropped and picked up throughout as main bobble motifs emerge.

about Clara Neep

It took hours of experimentation—guided by the memory of a grandmother's two-color bedspread still fresh in her mind—for Clara Neep to devise her own technique for changing colors without breaking threads. The result is her extraordinary bedspread design, a sharp departure from the more conventional color tones typical of most crochet. Clara has crocheted since childhood, when her older sister taught her the basic stitches, and has stuck to it as a hobby ever since—although, remarkably, she "has never learned to read instructions, and still does not do too well at it."

SIZE About 95" x 110".

MATERIALS J. & P. Coats Knit-Cro-Sheen, 129 (175-yd.) balls white No. 1 (color W) and 67 balls black No. 12 (B) (see adjoining note); steel crochet hook size 7 **or the size that will give you the correct gauge.**

Corner Square (1) 215 yds. white, 110 yds. black.

Side Rectangle (2) 325 yds. white, 165 yds. black.

Center Square (3) 485 yds. white, 250 yds. black.

Divide total for each color by 175 yds. (the amount in each ball) to determine the number of balls needed.

Before beginning work on individual units, see second NOTE, below right.

CORNER SQUARE (make 4): Starting at center with W, ch 6. Join with sl st to form ring. **1st rnd** Ch 3 (counts as 1 dc), work 2 dc in ring, ch 3, (work 3 dc in ring, ch 3) 3 times; drop W, attach B; join with sl st in top of ch 3. **2nd rnd** Sl st in each dc and ch around; drop B, pick up W; sl st in first sl st. **3rd rnd** Ch 3, dc in next 3 sts; work (2 dc, ch 3 and 2 dc) in next st (corner made);* dc in next 5 sts, work corner. Repeat from * twice more; dc in next st; drop W, pick up B; join. **4th rnd** Repeat 2nd rnd. **5th rnd** Ch 3, dc in next 6 sts, work corner, (dc in next 11 sts, work corner) 3 times; dc in next 4 sts; drop W, pick up B; join. **6th rnd** Repeat 2nd rnd. **7th rnd** Ch 3, dc in next 9 sts, work corner, (dc in next 17 sts, work corner) 3 times; dc in next 7 sts; drop W, pick up B; join. **8th rnd** Repeat 2nd rnd. **9th rnd** Ch 3, dc in next 12 sts, work corner, (dc in next 23 sts, work corner) 3 times; dc in next 10 sts; drop W, pick up B; join.

Continue in this manner, alternating B sl st rows and W dc rows and working 6 more dc on each side on each subsequent dc row, until 19 rows have been completed.

20th row With B, work until sl sts over ch sts of first corner have been completed, work bobble (b) in next st as follows: Sl st in next st, ch 3, (yo, insert hook in same st and draw lp through, yo and draw through 2 lps on hook) 5 times, yo and draw through all 6 lps on hook, ch 1 tightly, ch 3 (b made), sl st in each st to within 9 sts of next ch-3 sp, make b, sl st to 8 sts after ch-3 sp, make b, sl st to 1 st before the next ch-3 sp, make b, sl st around; join. **21st row** Ch 3, work W dc row in usual manner, working sl st in top of each B. **22nd row** With B, * sl st to 2 sts of sl st over b, make b, sl st in next dc, next sl st and next dc, make b. Repeat from * 3 times, sl st in each remaining dc or ch around; join. **23rd row** Ch 3, work W dc row in usual manner, working sl st in top of each b and 3 dc between b's.

NOTE *If you wish to make a different-size spread, each corner square (numbered 1 in Diagram 4, page 191) is 10" square, each side rectangle (numbered 2) 10" x 15" and each center square (numbered 3) 15" square. Working with these dimensions, make a chart to determine how many of each square or rectangle will be required for the desired size.*

To determine the thread quantities needed, multiply the number of squares by the amount of each color needed for each square (see specifications below Materials list).

NOTE *Work in back lp only of each sl st and dc throughout unless otherwise specified.*

Continue in this manner, following Diagram 1 for placement of diamond bobbles until 25 rows have been completed. On 26th row, work 1st row of large diamond b's (see diagram for placement of first b). Continue, following diagram until 37 rows have been completed. Break off.

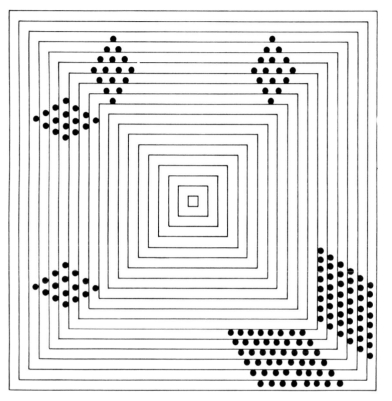

DIAGRAM 1

SIDE RECTANGLE (make 22): Starting at center with W, ch 42. **1st rnd** Dc in 4th ch from hook and in each of next 4 ch, ch 1, sk next ch, (dc in next 3 ch, ch 1, sk next ch) 7 times, dc in next 5 ch, ch 3; join with sl st in first ch of starting ch (base of last dc just worked). **2nd rnd** Working along opposite side of starting chain with B, sl st in first 5 ch, make b variation as follows: Sl st in next skipped ch, ch 3, (yo, insert hook in same st and draw lp through, yo and draw through 2 lps on hook) 5 times, yo and draw through all 6 lps on hook, sl st in front lp of skipped ch on 1st rnd, ch 3 (b variation made); (sl st in next ch on starting chain, make b in next ch, sl st in next ch, make b variation in next ch) 7 times, sl st in next 5 ch; sl st in each of 3 ch at end; work along opposite side as follows: Sl st in next 7 sts, make b, (sl

st in next 3 sts, make b) 6 times, sl st in next 7 sts; sl st in 3 ch at end; drop B, attach W; sl st in first sl st. **3rd rnd** Ch 3, dc in next 4 sl sts, dc in next sl st at base of b variation, (dc in next sl st, dc in top of next b, dc in next sl st, dc in sl st at base of next b variation) 7 times; work corner in next sl st, dc in next sl st, work corner in next sl st; dc in next 7 sl st, dc in top of next b, (dc in next 3 sl st, dc in top of next b) 6 times, dc in next 7 sl st; work corner in next sl st, dc in next ch, work corner in next sl st; drop W, pick up B; sl st in top of ch-3. **4th rnd** Sl st in each st around; drop B, pick up W; sl st in first sl st.

Continue in same manner as for Corner Square, following Diagram 2 for completion of center b diamond and for placement of remaining b diamonds.

DIAGRAM 2

CENTER SQUARE (make 30): Work as for Corner Square through first 3 rnds. **4th rnd** (Work b in next st, sl st in next 11 sts) 4 times, drop B, pick up W; sl st in top of ch-3.

Continue in this manner, following Diagram 3 for placement of b's.

FINISHING Follow Diagram 4 for placement. With right sides together, using B, sl st adjacent edges together, working through back lp only of corresponding sts.

Edging: 1st rnd With W, work dc around entire spread, working corner at each corner; join. Break off. **2nd rnd** With B, sl st in each st around; join. Break off.

1	2	2	2	2	2	1
2	3	3	3	3	3	2
2	3	3	3	3	3	2
2	3	3	3	3	3	2
2	3	3	3	3	3	2
2	3	3	3	3	3	2
2	3	3	3	3	3	2
1	2	2	2	2	2	1

DIAGRAM 4

DIAGRAM 3

SAILBOATS AND NAUTICAL FLAGS

A crocheted bedspread by Deanna Rosenkranz of Shaker Heights, Ohio

In this banner-bold bedspread, afghan stitch, crochet and cross-stitch join up to create a seagoing theme of nautical flags, sailboats and wavy borders.

about Deanna Rosenkranz

As a professional artist, Deanna Rosenkranz particularly enjoys puzzling out original patterns, ''experimenting with new techniques and stitches in crocheting afghans of my own design.'' That enthusiasm for originality, combined with the sadly limited selection of commercial bedspreads, provides ample incentive to pursue her creative specialty. Each finished work brings a special sense of accomplishment because, explains Deanna, ''as the mother of seven children, my time is limited to brief moments of this relaxing activity.''

SIZE About 50″ x 80″. Each sailboat block measures 15″ x 19″; each flag block measures 7½″ x 10½″.

MATERIALS Knitting worsted: 16 ozs. each of red (R) and blue ombré (O), 12 ozs. each of white (W) and blue (B); aluminum afghan hook size K and aluminum crochet hook size K (or both in international hook size 7.00 mm) **or the size that will give you the correct gauge;** large-eyed yarn needle.

GAUGE In afghan st, 7 sts = 2″; 3 rows = 1″. In sc and dc, 7 sts = 2″.

BLOCK A (make 2): See instructions for Afghan Stitch, page 248. With B and afghan hook, ch 29 to measure about 8½″. Work in afghan st of 29 lps (28 sts — first lp is not a st), working colors as follows: Work 3 rows with B. **4th row** Work 4 sts B, attach W and work 20 sts W, attach another B and work 4 sts B. **5th and 6th rows** Work 4 B sts, 20 W sts, 4 B sts. **7th row** Work 4 B sts, 5 W, attach R and work 10 R, attach another W and work 5 W, work 4 B. **8th, 9th and 10th rows** Work 4 B, 5 W, 10 R, 5 W and 4 B. Break off R and 2nd W. **11th, 12th and 13th rows** Work 4 B, 20 W and 4 B. Break off W and extra B. Now work 3 rows with B only. Sl st in each st across. Break off.

Block border: 1st rnd Attach O to one corner. Using O and crochet hook, and with right side of work facing you, ch 3 (first dc), work 2 dc in same place where O was joined, then work around in dc, working a dc in each st or end of each row and working 3 dc at each corner. Sl st to top of beg ch-3. Break off O; attach R. **2nd rnd** Using R and crochet hook, and with right side of work facing you, ch 1, sc in each st around, working 3 sc at each corner. Break off.

BLOCK B (make 2): With B and afghan hook, ch 29 to measure about 8½″. Work in afghan st of 29 lps (28 sts), working colors as follows: Work 5 rows with B. Break off B; attach W. Work 6 rows with W. Break off W; attach B. Work 5 rows with B. Sl st in each st across. Break off.

Work block border same as for Block A.

BLOCK C (make 2): With R and afghan hook, ch 14 to measure about 4½″; drop R; attach W and ch 15 more with W (total chain measures about 8½″). Work in afghan st of 29 lps (28 sts), working colors as follows: **1st through 8th rows** Work 14 W sts, 14 R. Break off W and R. **9th row** Attach R and work 14 R; attach W and work 14 W. **10th through 16th rows** Work 14 R, 14 W. Matching colors, sl st in each st across. Break off.

Work block border same as for Block A.

NOTE *Afghan is crocheted in 4 sailboat and 16 flag blocks, each with design area worked in afghan stitch, border added in crochet stitches. Blocks are assembled, then ripple border is crocheted in strips and added to assembled blocks with the corners mitered and sewn.*

BLOCK D (make 2): With B and afghan hook, ch 29 to measure about 8½". Work in afghan st of 29 lps (28 sts), working colors as follows: Work 3 rows with B. Break off B; attach W. Work 3 rows with W. Break off W; attach R. Work 4 rows with R. Break off R; attach W. Work 3 rows with W. Break off W; attach B. Work 3 rows with B. Sl st in each st across. Break off.

Work block border same as for Block A.

BLOCK E (make 2): With R and afghan hook, ch 29 to measure about 8½". Work in afghan st of 29 lps (28 sts), working colors as follows: Work 8 rows with R. Break off R; attach B. Work 8 rows with B. Sl st in each st across. Break off.

Work block border same as for Block A.

BLOCK F (make 2): With W and afghan hook, ch 14 to measure 4½"; drop W; attach R and ch 15 more with R (total chain measures about 8½"). Work in afghan st of 29 lps (28 sts), working colors as follows: **All 16 rows** Work 14 R sts, 14 W. Matching colors, sl st in each st across. Break off.

Work block border same as for Block A.

BLOCK G (make 2): With B and afghan hook, ch 29 to measure about 8½". Work in afghan st of 29 lps (28 sts), working colors as follows: Work 5 rows with B. **6th row** Work 7 B sts, attach W and work 14 W, attach another B and work 7 B. **7th through 11th rows** Work 7 B sts, 14 W, 7 B. Break off W and second B. Now work 5 rows with B only. Sl st in each st across. Break off.

Work block border same as for Block A.

BLOCK H (make 2): With R and afghan hook, ch 9; drop R; attach W and ch 10 more with W; drop W, attach another B and ch 10 more with B (total chain measures about 8½"). Work in afghan st of 29 lps (28 sts), working colors as follows: **All 16 rows** Work 9 sts B, 10 W, 9 R. Matching colors, sl st in each st across. Break off.

Work block border same as for Block A.

Each square = one stitch

Each square = one stitch

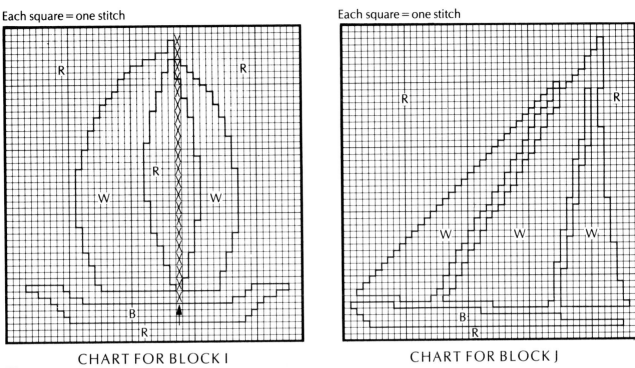

CHART FOR BLOCK I

CHART FOR BLOCK J

⊠ cross stitch

↑ indicates start of embroidery

NOTE *For method of winding pull balls, see page 255.*

BLOCK I With R and afghan hook, ch 48 to measure about 12½″. Work in afghan st of 48 lps (47 sts) and follow Chart for Block I for design. Attach a separate ball of yarn for each separate area of color so that you do not carry colors across back of work. When a color area is completed, break off yarn.

When last row of chart is completed, sl st in each st across. Break off. Work block border same as for Block A.

BLOCK J Work in same manner as for Block I, but follow Chart for Block J for design.

BLOCK K Work in same manner as for Block I, but follow Chart for Block K for design.

BLOCK L Work in same manner as for Block I, but follow Chart for Block L for design.

EMBROIDERY (blocks I, K and L): Thread strand of O in yarn needle. See instructions for working Cross-stitch over Afghan Stitch, page 249. Beginning just above arrow on chart, work cross-stitches straight up indicated stitch to top row, making each cross-stitch a single stitch in width and 2 stitches in length as indicated on chart.

Each square = one stitch

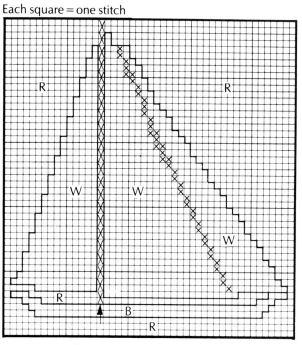

CHART FOR BLOCK K

- ☒ red
- ☒ cross stitch
- ↑ indicates start of embroidery

Each square = one stitch

- ☒ cross stitch
- ↑ indicates start of embroidery

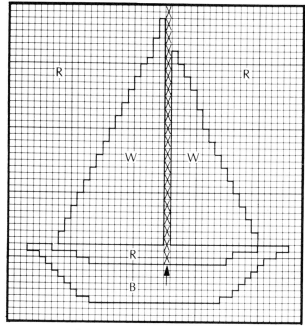

CHART FOR BLOCK L

PLACEMENT DIAGRAM

ASSEMBLING Following Placement Diagram, using crochet hook and R, sl st blocks together on right side of work, forming a ridge at joinings. **NOTE** *All blocks are joined upside-down on lower half of diagram for symmetry.*

RIPPLE BORDER: Narrow ends (make 2 strips): With W and crochet hook, ch 164. **1st row** (right side): With W, sc in 2nd ch from hook, sc in next 3 ch, 3 sc in next ch, * sc in next 4 ch, sk 2 ch, sc in next 4 ch, 3 sc in next ch. Repeat from * across to last 4 ch, sc in last 4 ch. Break off W; attach B. With B, ch 1, turn. **2nd row** With B, working in *front* lp only of each st, sk first sc, * sc in next 4 sc, 3 sc in next sc, sc in next 4 sc, sk 2 sc, sc in next 4 sc. Repeat from * across, ending with sc in next 4 sc, sk last sc. Ch 1, turn. **3rd row** With B and working in *back* lp only of each st, work same as for 2nd row. Break off B; attach O. With O, ch 1, turn. **4th and 5th rows** With O, work same as for 2nd and 3rd rows. Ch 1, turn. **6th row** With O, work same as for 2nd row. Break off O; attach W. With W, ch 3, turn. **7th row** With W and working in *back* lp only of each st, sk first sc, * dc in next 4 sc, 3 dc in next sc, dc in next 4 sc, sk 2 sc, dc in next 4 sc. Repeat from * across, ending with dc in next 4 sc, sk last sc. Break off W; attach B. With B, ch 1, turn. **8th row** With B, working in *front* lp only, sk first dc, * sc in next 4 dc, 3 sc in next dc, sc in next 4 dc, skip 2 dc, sc in next 4 dc. Repeat from * across, ending with sc in next 4 dc, sk last dc. Ch 1, turn. **9th row** With B, repeat 3rd row. Break off B; attach R. With R, ch 1, turn. **10th row** With R and working in both lps, sc in each sc across. Ch 3, turn. **11th row** With R and working in both lps, dc in first sc, * hdc in next 3 sc, sc in next 3 sc (over high point), hdc in next 3 sc, dc in next 2 sc (in dip). Repeat from * across, ending with hdc in next 3 sc, dc in last sc. Break off.

Side edges (make 2 strips): With W and crochet hook, ch 263. Work same as for Narrow Ends until 9th row is completed. Break off B. Mark dip between 7th and 8th high points from each end (this should be about 22″ in from each end with 11 high points lying between markers).

On wrong side of work, attach O at first marker. Now work only between the two markers. **10th and 11th rows** With O, work same as 2nd and 3rd rows. Ch 1, turn. **12th row** With O, work same as for 2nd row. Break off O; attach W. With W, ch 3, turn. **13th row** With W, work same as 7th row. Break off W; attach B. **14th row** With B, work same as 3rd row. Break off B; attach O. With O, ch 1, turn. **15th and 16th rows** With O, repeat 2nd and 3rd rows. **17th row** With O, repeat 2nd row. Break off O; attach W. With W, ch 3,

turn. **18th row** With W, repeat 7th row. Break off W; attach R to end of 9th row (last long row worked). With R, ch 3. **19th row** Start at edge and work across 9th row to added section between markers as follows: With R and working in both lps, dc in first dc, * hdc in next 3 dc, sc in next 3 dc (over high point), hdc in next 3 dc, dc in next 2 dc (in dip). Repeat from * across, ending with hdc in next 3 dc, dc in last dc **; turn work sideways and work sc along side edge of added section, spacing sts to keep edge of work smooth and flat; turn work to work across last row of added section as follows: Dc in first dc, then repeat from * to ** once; turn work sideways and work sc along side edge as before to marker; turn work to work across remaining portion of 9th row as follows: Dc in first dc, repeat from * to **. Break off.

JOINING RIPPLE BORDER Pin border to assembled block section, centering each border strip and fitting added section carefully into place at sides. About 5½″ of border strip will extend at each corner end. With crochet hook and R, sl st border to block section on right side of work, forming ridge at joining. **Mitered corners** Pin seamline for mitered corners diagonally across strip end from inner corner to outer corner of border. Sew neatly on wrong side. Fold excess triangular strip ends away from seam on wrong side and sew neatly in place.

PART 3 Knitted Designs

For basic knitting instructions and reminders about techniques, see page 250.

SAMPLER IN PASTELS

*A knitted afghan by
Bernice L. Hampson of
San Clemente, California*

*Vivid aqua, yellow and salmon pink
are set against a cream ground in
this stunning multi-textured and
multi-patterned afghan.*

*about
Bernice L. Hampson*

A dedicated knitter who "kept all twelve of my grandchildren in sweaters," Bernice Hampson displays exceptional talent for creating and combining her own pattern variations. In her superb winning entry, there are, all together, eight basic panels building out toward the top, bottom and the sides from a central rectangle (see the diagram for this ingenious "building block" placement). Each change of color is done in a two-row plan, quite different from the Scandinavian method of carrying yarn behind the work on the wrong side and, in Bernice's own words, "not hard to do." Her knitted afghan, in its marvelous complexity, is certain to both challenge and charm the experienced knitter.

SIZE About 62" x 76".

MATERIALS Knitting worsted: 64 ozs. cream (color A), 6 ozs. each bright aqua (B), salmon pink (C) and yellow (D); you will need one or four (see NOTE below right) 36"-long circular knitting needles No. 7 (or English needles No. 6) **or the size that will give you the correct gauge.**

GAUGE 9 sts = 2" in stockinette st. Gauge will vary with patterns. Finished size for each section is given at the beginning of directions for each pattern.

FOUR-NEEDLE AFGHAN Referring to diagram, start at edge X and work Pattern 1 (see One-needle Afghan, p.204, for this pattern) on one circular needle. Do not bind off at end, but keep sts on needle. Inc 1 st and work Pattern 2 at top of Pattern 1, starting with 1st row on right side of work. When pattern has been completed, leave sts on needle and, with right side facing you, turn work upside down. With second circular needle and color A, pick up needed sts along cast-on edge (X) of Pattern 1 and work Pattern 2 again at bottom of Pattern 1, starting with 2nd (wrong side) row. At

NOTE *This afghan is suggested for experienced knitters.*

NOTE *Our directions are written to enable you to make each different pattern section separately for ease in handling. The original afghan, however, was made in one continuous piece by working back and forth on four separate circular needles.*

If you wish to make each pattern separately by working back and forth on one circular needle, follow directions under One-needle Afghan. If you wish to make afghan in one continuous piece with four needles, work as directed under Four-needle Afghan.

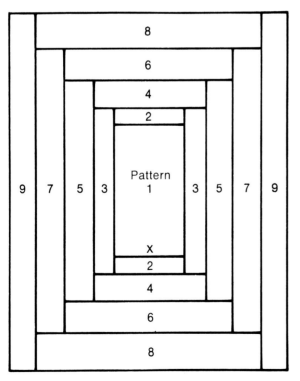

PLACEMENT DIAGRAM

completion of pattern, leave sts on needle and turn work sideways. With third circular needle, pick up needed sts for Pattern 3 along right edge of Patterns 2, 1 and 2 and work Pattern 3, starting this and all following patterns with 1st row on *wrong* side of work. Leave sts on needle. Turn work and, with fourth needle, work Pattern 3 again along opposite edge in same manner.

With first needle (74 sts), pick up 28 additional sts along one narrow end of one Pattern 3 section and 29 additional sts along narrow end of other Pattern 3 section to make up needed sts on first needle in order to work wider Pattern 4. Then work opposite Pattern 4 in same manner with second needle.

Continue to work each section in this manner, picking up with each point of circular needle the additional sts across narrow ends of last 2 sections made. Work Patterns 5 with third and fourth needles, Patterns 6 with first and second needles, Patterns 7 with third and fourth needles, and so on to complete afghan.

ONE-NEEDLE AFGHAN Pattern 1 Make one 15″ x 27″ section. Refer to diagram as you work. Starting at edge X, with A, cast on 73 sts. **1st through 4th row** (K 1 row, p 1 row) twice. At end of 4th row, drop A; attach B. **5th row (right side)** With B, k across. **6th row** With B, k 5, * (work long k st as follows: Insert needle into next st as if to k, wrap yarn around tip of needle 3 times, draw needle through to complete st — 3 lps on needle) 3 times; k 7. Repeat from * across, ending last repeat k 5. Break off B; pick up A. (**Note** From now on, when slipping sts, hold yarn in back on right-side rows and in front on wrong-side rows.) **7th row** With A, k 1, * sl 1, k 3, (sl 1 dropping extra 2 lps) 3 times; k 3. Repeat from * across, ending sl 1, k 1. **8th row** With A, p 1, * sl 1, p 3, sl 3, p 3. Repeat from * across, ending sl 1, p 1. **9th row** With A, k 5, * sl 3, k 7. Repeat from * across, ending k 5. **10th row** With A, p 5, * sl 3, p 7. Repeat from * across, ending p 5. **11th row** With A, k 3, * sl 2, drop next st from needle to front of work, sl same 2 sl sts back onto left needle point, pick up dropped st and k it, k 3, drop next st from needle to front of work, k 2, pick up dropped st and k it, k 3. Repeat from * across. Drop A; attach C. **12th row (wrong side)** With C, p 1, sl 2, * (work p 1, k 1 and p 1 in next st, then sl 2) twice; work p 1, k 1 and p 1 in next st, then sl 3. Repeat from * across, ending (p 1, k 1 and p 1 in next st, then sl 2) 3 times; p 1. **13th row** With C, k 1, sl 2, * make bobble in next 3 sts as follows: P 3, turn, k 3, turn, sl 1, k 2

tog, psso — bobble completed; (sl 2, make bobble) twice; sl 3. Repeat from * across, ending (making bobble, sl 2) 3 times; k 1. Break off C; pick up A. **14th row** With A, p. across. **15th through 25th rows** Repeat 1st through 11th rows. At end of 25th row, drop A; attach D. **26th and 27th rows** With D, work as for 12th and 13th rows. Break off D; pick up A. **28th row** With A, p across.

Repeat these 28 rows 5 times more, then repeat 1st through 18th rows once more, ending with wrong-side row. Bind off.

Pattern 2 Make two 3½" x 15" sections. Work with color A throughout. Cast on 74 sts. **1st row (right side)** K across. **2nd row** K across. **3rd row** K 1, make long k st as for Pattern 1 in each st across, ending k 1. **4th row** K 1, * (sl first lp of next long st as if to p, drop 2nd and 3rd lps of same st) 4 times; sl these 4 sts back onto left needle point; insert right needle point through all 4 long sts as if to k, work k 1, p 1, k 1 and p 1 in all 4 sts tog before dropping from left needle point. Repeat from * across, ending k 1. **5th and 6th rows** K across.

Repeat these 6 rows 3 times more, ending with a wrong-side row. Bind off.

Pattern 3 Make two 4½" x 34" sections. Work with color A throughout. Cast on 169 sts. **1st and 2nd rows** K across. **3rd row (wrong side)** P across. **4th and 5th rows** K across. **6th row** K 1, * make long k st as for Pattern 1 in each of next 5 sts, k 1. Repeat from * across. **7th row** K 1, * work sl cl st in next 5 sts as follows: Bring yarn to front of work, (sl first lp of next st as if to p, drop 2nd and 3rd lps of same st) 5 times, bring yarn to back of work, (sl all 5 long sts back onto left needle point, bring yarn to front of work, sl 5 long sts onto right needle point, bring yarn to back of work — yarn is wrapped around 5 long lps) twice — sl cl st completed; k 1. Repeat from * across. **8th through 10th rows** K across. **11th row** P across. **12th and 13th rows** K across. **14th row** K 4, * make long k st in each of next 5 sts, k 1. Repeat from * across, ending k 4. **15th row** K 4, * work sl cl st in next 5 long sts, k 1. Repeat from * across, ending last repeat k 4. **16th and 17th rows** K across.

Repeat 2nd through 12th rows once more. Bind off.

Pattern 4 Make two 5½" x 24" sections. With A, cast on 131 sts. **1st and 2nd rows** K across. **3rd row (wrong side)** P across. Drop A; attach C. **4th and 5th rows** With C, k across. Drop C; attach B. (**Note** From now on, when slipping sts, hold yarn in back on right-side rows and in front on wrong-side rows.) **6th row** With B, k 1, * sl 1, k 1. Repeat

from * across. **7th row** With B, k 1, * sl 1, k 1. Repeat from * across. Break off B; pick up C. **8th and 9th rows** With C, k across. Break off C; pick up A. **10th row** With A, k 2, * sl 1, k 1. Repeat from * across, ending last repeat k 2. **11th row** With A, p 2, * sl 1, p 1. Repeat from * across, ending last repeat p 2. **12th row** With A, k across. **13th row** With A, p across. **14th and 15th rows** Repeat 12th and 13th rows. Drop A; attach D. **16th and 17th rows** With D, k across. Drop D; attach B. **18th and 19th rows** With B, repeat 6th and 7th rows. Break off B; pick up D. **20th and 21st rows** With D, k across. Break off D; pick up A. **22nd through 25th rows** With A, repeat 10th through 13th rows.

Repeat 2nd through 25th rows once more. Bind off.

Pattern 5 Make two 6″ x 45″ sections. With A, cast on 224 sts. **1st and 2nd rows** K across. **3rd row (wrong side)** P across. Drop A; attach B. See Note before 6th row on Pattern 4. **4th row** With B, k 1, * sl 2, k 8. Repeat from * across, ending sl 2, k 1. Drop B; attach D. **5th row** With D, p 1, sl 3, * p 6, sl 4. Repeat from * across, ending p 6, sl 3, p 1. **6th row** With D, k 1, sl 3, * k 6, sl 4. Repeat from * across, ending k 6, sl 3, k 1. Break off D; pick up B. **7th row** With B, p 1, * sl 2, p 8. Repeat from * across, ending sl 2, p 1. Drop B; pick up A. **8th row** With A, k across. **9th row** With A, p across. Drop A; pick up B. **10th row** With B, k 6, * sl 2, k 8. Repeat from * across, ending last repeat k 6. Drop B; attach C. **11th row** With C, p 5, * sl 4, p 6. Repeat from * across, ending last repeat p 5. **12th row** With C, k 5, * sl 4, k 6. Repeat from * across, ending last repeat k 5. Break off C; pick up B. **13th row** With B, p 6, * sl 2, p 8. Repeat from * across, ending last repeat p 6. Drop B; pick up A.

Repeat 2nd through 13th rows twice more, then 2nd through 9th rows once again. Bind off.

Pattern 6 Make two 6½″ x 36″ sections. Work with color A throughout. Cast on 188 sts. **1st row (wrong side)** K across. **2nd row** P 7, * k 4, p 6. Repeat from * across, ending k 4, p 7. **3rd row** P 3, k 4, * p 4, k 6. Repeat from * to last 11 sts, then p 4, k 4, p 3. **4th row** Repeat 2nd row. **5th row** P 3, k 4, * yo twice, p 4, yo twice, k 6, p 4, k 6. Repeat from * across, ending last repeat k 4 instead of k 6; p 3. **6th row** P 7, * k 4, p 6, drop the 2 yo lps from left needle point to front of work without working them, k 4, drop the 2 yo lps from left needle point to front of work without working them. Repeat from * across, ending p 7. Insert free needle point into each pair of dropped lps and pull lps up until they are long enough to tie. Remove needle point and tie lps in square knot. **7th row**

Repeat 3rd row. **8th and 9th rows** Repeat 2nd and 3rd rows.
10th row Repeat 2nd row. **11th row** P 3, k 4, * p 4, k 6, yo
twice, p 4, yo twice, k 6. Repeat from * across, ending k 4,
p 3. **12th row** P 7, * drop yo lps, k 4, drop yo lps, p 6, k 4,
p 6. Repeat from * across, ending p 7. Tie lps as before. **13th
row** Repeat 3rd row.

Repeat 2nd through 13th rows once more, then 2nd
through 9th rows again. Bind off in pattern.

Pattern 7 Make two 6″ x 58″ sections. Work with color A
throughout. Cast on 282 sts. **1st row (wrong side)** K across.
2nd row K 11, * k 2 tog, yo, k 1, yo, sl 1, k 1, psso, k 10.
Repeat from * across, ending last repeat k 11. **3rd row** P 10,
* p 2 tog through back of lps, yo, p 3, yo, p 2 tog, p 8. Repeat
from * across, ending last repeat p 10. **4th row** K 9, * k 2
tog, yo, k 5, yo, sl 1, k 1, psso, k 6. Repeat from * across,
ending last repeat K 9. **5th row** P 8, * p 2 tog through back
of lps, yo, p 1, yo, p 2 tog, p 1, p 2 tog through back of lps,
yo, p 1, yo, p 2 tog, p 4. Repeat from * across, ending last
repeat p 8. **6th row** K 7, * k 2 tog, yo, k 3, yo, k 3 tog, yo,
k 3, yo, sl 1, k 1, psso, k 2. Repeat from * across, ending k
7. **7th row** P 8, * yo, p 5, yo, p 1, yo, p 5, yo, p 4 (4 sts inc
for each pattern repeat). Repeat from * across, ending last
repeat p 8. **8th row** K 9, * yo, sl 1, k 1, psso, k 1, k 2 tog,
yo, k 3, yo, sl 1, k 1, psso, k 1, k 2 tog, yo, k 6. Repeat from
* across, ending last repeat k 9. **9th row** P 10, * p 3 tog, yo,
p 5, yo, p 3 tog, p 8 (2 sts dec for each pattern repeat).
Repeat from * across, ending last repeat p 10. **10th row** K
12, * yo, sl 1, k 1, psso, k 1, k 2 tog, yo, k 12. Repeat from
* across. **11th row** P 9, * p 2 tog through back of lps, p 2,
yo, p 3 tog, yo, p 2, p 2 tog, p 6 (2 sts dec for each pattern
repeat). Repeat from * across, ending last repeat p 9.

Repeat 2nd through 11th rows 3 times more. Bind off.

Pattern 8 Make two 7½″ x 48″ sections. With A, cast on
243 sts. **1st and 2nd rows** K across. **3rd row (wrong side)**
P across. Drop A; attach B. **4th row** With B, k 1, * sl 1 with
yarn in front of work, k 1. Repeat from * across. **5th row**
With B, p across. Break off B; pick up A. **6th row** With A,
k 2, * sl 1 with yarn in front of work, k 1. Repeat from *
across, ending k 2. **7th row** With A, p across. Drop A; attach
C. (**Note** On next 4 rows, when slipping sts, hold yarn in
back on right-side rows, and in front on wrong-side rows).
8th row With C, k 1, * sl 1, k 3. Repeat from * across,
ending sl 1, k 1. **9th row** With C, p 1, * sl 1, p 3. Repeat
from * across, ending sl 1, p 1. **10th row** Repeat 8th row.
11th row Repeat 9th row. Break off C; pick up A. **12th**

through 17th rows Repeat 2nd through 7th rows. Drop A; attach D. **18th through 21st rows** With D, repeat 8th through 11th rows. Break off D; pick up A.

Repeat 2nd through 21st rows once more, then 2nd through 7th rows again. Bind off.

Pattern 9 Make two 5½" x 73" sections. With A, cast on 369 sts. **1st through 3rd rows** With A, k across. Drop A; attach B. **4th row (right side)** With B, k 2, * sl 1, k 1; work k 1, yo, k 1, yo and k 1 all in next st; k 1. Repeat from * across, ending sl 1, k 2. **5th row** With B, k 2, * sl 1, k 1, (make long st as follows: P next st wrapping yarn around needle twice) 5 times; k 1. Repeat from * across, ending sl 1, k 2. Break off B; pick up A. **6th row** With A, k 4, * (sl first lp of next long st as if to k, drop 2nd lp of same st) 5 times; k 3. Repeat from * across, ending k 4. **7th row** With A, k 4, * sl 5, k 3. Repeat from * across, ending k 4. **8th row** With A, k 3, * k 2 tog, sl 3, then sl 1, k 1, psso, k 1. Repeat from * across, ending k 3. **9th row** With A, k 3, * p 1, sl 3, p 1, k 1. Repeat from * across, ending k 3. **10th row** With A, k 3, * k 2 tog, sl 1, then sl 1, k 1, psso, k 1. Repeat from * across, ending k 3. **11th row** With A, k 3, * p 1, sl 1, p 1, k 1. Repeat from * across, ending last repeat k 3. **12th row** With A, k 4, * k 1 in back lp, k 3. Repeat from * across, ending last repeat k 4. **13th row** With A, k 4, * p 1 in back lp, k 3. Repeat from * across, ending last repeat k 4. Drop A; attach C. **14th row** With C, k 2; * work k 1, yo, k 1, yo and k 1 all in next st; k 1, sl 1, k 1. Repeat from * to last 3 sts, then work k 1, yo, k 1, yo and k 1 all in next st; k 2. **15th row** With C, k 2, * (make long st as for 5th row) 5 times; k 1, sl 1, k 1. Repeat from * across, ending with 5 long sts; k 2. Break off C; pick up A. **16th row** With A, k 2, * (sl first lp of next long st as if to k, drop 2nd lp of same st) 5 times; k 3. Repeat from * across, ending k 2. **17th row** With A, k 2, * sl 5, k 3. Repeat from * across, ending k 2. **18th row** With A, k 1, * k 2 tog, sl 3, then sl 1, k 1, psso, k 1. Repeat from * across. **19th row** With A, k 1, * p 1, sl 3, p 1, k 1. Repeat from * across. **20th row** With A, k 1, * k 2 tog, sl 1, then sl 1, k 1, psso, k 1. Repeat from * across. **21st row** With A, k 1, * p 1, sl 1, p 1, k 1. Repeat from * across. **22nd row** With A, k 2, * k 1 in back lp, k 3. Repeat from * across, ending k 2. **23rd row** With A, k 2, * p 1 in back lp, k 3. Repeat from * across, ending k 2. Drop A; attach D. **24th and 25th rows** With D, repeat 4th and 5th rows. Break off D; pick up A. **26th through 33rd rows** With A, repeat 6th through 13th rows. Drop A; attach C. **34th and 35th rows** With C, repeat 14th

and 15th rows. Break off C; pick up A. **36th through 43rd rows** With A, repeat 16th through 23rd rows. Drop A; attach B. **44th and 45th rows** With B, repeat 4th and 5th rows. Break off B; pick up A. **46th through 53rd rows** With A, repeat 6th through 13th rows.

Bind off.

FINISHING Block separate sections to measurements given. Neatly sew or crochet edges together, following diagram and starting with Pattern 1, adding Pattern 2, then 3, 4 and so on.

Border With right side of work facing you, using color A, pick up and k 370 sts along one long edge of afghan. **1st row (wrong side)** K across. **2nd row** K 1, yo, k to last st, yo, k 1. **3rd row** P 1, k to last st, p 1. **4th row** K 1, * yo, k 2 tog. Repeat from * to last st, yo, k 1. **5th row** Repeat 3rd row. **6th through 9th rows** Repeat 2nd and 3rd rows twice more. Bind off. Repeat along opposite long edge. Pick up and k 294 sts along each short edge and work in same manner.

Sew mitered corners together neatly.

TAOS SUNRISE

A knitted afghan by Gloria L. Morris of Pittsburg, Kansas

Straight knitting, with careful control of the tension on the variegated yarn, produced this undulating pattern of shimmering colors. Afghan is done in three separate panels, which are then joined together.

about
Gloria L. Morris

"I love working with variegated yarn because of the beautiful designs that emerge," explains Gloria Morris. "I also love anything Mexican — the color, design and freedom of expression." That is why she chose, for her contest entry, a variegated yarn in hues that suggest the Mexican landscape, and then, by her own self-taught method of controlling color patterns through tension on the yarn, worked toward a design that would capitalize on their warmth. She plans to use her afghan herself, "because over the years I have made probably fifteen or twenty afghans and have given them all away!" But, she goes on to say, "they are all appreciated, and that is payment of the best kind."

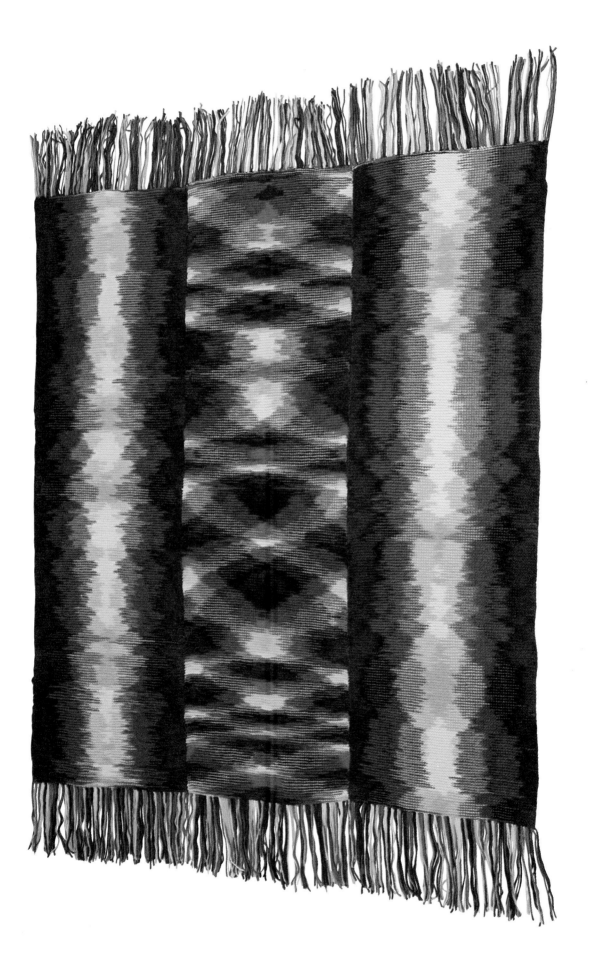

NOTE *Afghan is knitted in three panels, each 19" wide. Color pattern is formed automatically by yarn when proper tension is applied as explained in directions.*

SIZE About 57" x 60", plus 8" fringe at each end.

MATERIALS Red Heart Mexicana Ombré, 12 (3½-oz.) skeins; 1 pair size 7 knitting needles (or size 6 English needles) **or the size that will give you the correct gauge;** aluminum crochet hook size F (or international size 4.00 mm).

GAUGE About 4 sts = 1". Tension will vary slightly as you work panels (explained at appropriate points in directions below).

CENTER PANEL Cast on 80 sts. Work in garter st (k each row), with even tension, allowing colors to fall as they will, until panel measures 60". Bind off all sts.

SIDE PANELS (make 2): Cast on 80 sts. Work in garter st until yellow section of yarn falls exactly in middle of row. Then continue in garter st, controlling tension on yarn to keep warm colors (yellow and orange) in the center of the panel with the cooler shades (blue and purple) at each end. Colors may shift slightly, which adds interest to the pattern, but warm colors should generally be centered to retain the desired effect. The designer suggests that some knitters may find that it works better to cast on 82 stitches for this panel than the 80 stitches specified.

Knit until panel measures same as center panel. Bind off all sts.

FINISHING Crochet or sew panels together. Crochet a row of sc all around afghan, spacing sts to keep edges smooth and flat. **Fringe** Cut a 16" strand for each fringe. Fold in half; with crochet hook, draw folded end from front to wrong side through sc at narrow end of afghan; pull cut ends through loop and tighten. Make fringes in this manner along both narrow ends of afghan.

MAPLE LEAVES

A knitted afghan by Mrs. Barney Haury of Medina, Ohio

All the glorious colors of turning leaves at the peak of the fall season radiate from this spectacular work.

about Mrs. Barney Haury

"Living in Ohio, my favorite season of the year is autumn, with all its beautiful warm colors on display for so short a time," writes Mrs. Barney Haury. "My inspiration was to capture those colors in an afghan I could enjoy all winter long." Her objective clearly set, Mrs. Haury planned the design for her prize-winning afghan, collecting real leaves for her patterns and choosing yarn scraps that would suggest the rich and varied natural shades of foliage in the fall. After keeping eight grandchildren in hand-knitted sweaters and giving away thirty afghans, "now," she says, "I really enjoy creating my own designs."

SIZE About 44″ x 56″. Each leaf block measures 7¾″ x 10½″.

MATERIALS Knitting worsted: 20 ozs. dark brown (color A), 16 ozs. brown tweed (B); small amounts of knitting worsted in leaf shades — yellows, oranges, reds, browns and greens (see adjoining NOTE); 1 pair size 8 knitting needles (or size 5 English needles), **or the size that will give you the correct gauge;** aluminum crochet hook size F (or international size 4.00 mm); tapestry needle.

GAUGE 5 sts ⪉ 1″; 7 rows = 1″.

NOTE *On original afghan, the colors used were different for each block. They are listed on page 218 as a guide, with the suggestion that rather than try to duplicate the colors exactly, you simply use scraps and remnants already on hand, or easily (and cheaply) obtained from knitting friends or local yarn shops.*

Attach bobbins or small balls of yarn as needed to work design (see Knitting with Pull Balls, page 255); do not carry colors across back of work. When changing colors, twist new strand under old to prevent holes in work.

LEAF BLOCKS Make 28 blocks with varying colors for leaves. With A, cast on 52 sts. Work seed st for 4 rows. **Next row (right side)** Work 4 sts in seed st (border); attach B and k 44 B (first row of chart); attach another A and work 4 sts A in seed st as established (border). **Following row** With A, work 4 border sts in seed st, p 44 B (2nd row of chart), with A work 4 border sts in seed st. Continue in this manner, working first and last 4 sts in A seed st for border, and center 44 sts in stockinette st, following chart for design. Work from X to Y on k rows, from Y to X on p rows and up to Z in length, adding desired leaf color pull balls as needed. When

Each square = one stitch

A = brown tweed
B = leaf color

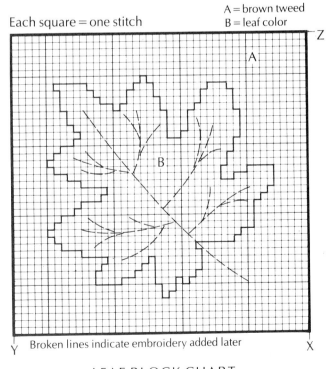

Broken lines indicate embroidery added later

LEAF BLOCK CHART

last row of chart is completed, break off B and with A only, work 4 rows in seed st. Bind off all sts in seed st.

FINISHING Block leaf blocks to measurement. **Embroidery** Thread a contrasting-color yarn in tapestry needle and with outline st (see Embroidery Stitches, page 241), embroider vein lines on each leaf (indicated by broken lines on chart).

Following Placement Diagram for general arrangement of colors and for the direction of leaves, sew blocks together neatly. Attach A to one corner and, with right side of work facing you, crochet a row of sc all around afghan, having the number of sts on each side between corner sc a multiple of 5 sc, plus 1 (such as 216 or 221 or 226 sts), spacing sts to keep edges smooth and flat. **Next row** Work sc in sc, * sk 1 sc, work 6 dc in next sc (shell made), skip 2 sc, sc in next sc. Repeat from * around, working shell at each corner. Break off.

COLOR KEY (original afghan)

BLOCK	LEAF COLOR	EMBROIDERY COLOR
A	maroon	gray
B	lime	avocado
C	pale orange	burnt orange
D	gold	yellow
E	yellow	mustard
F	dark orange	copper
G	copper	brown
H	red orange	maroon
I	red	maroon
J	camel	copper
K	orange	red orange
L	gold orange	brown
M	pale maroon	maroon
N	camel	brown
O	yellow	mustard
P	avocado	pale olive
Q	burnt orange	tan
R	red	maroon
S	pale olive	avocado
T	pale yellow	mustard
U	lime	dark lime
V	mustard	brown
W	yellow	gold
X	red orange	orange
Y	yellow green	mustard
Z	green	olive
AA	tan	brown
BB	maroon	black

A ↑	B ↓	C ↑	D ↓
E ↕	F ↑	G ↓	H ↑
I ↑	J ↓	K ↑	L ↓
M ↕	N ↑	O ↓	P ↑
Q ↑	R ↓	S ↑	T ↓
U ↕	V ↑	W ↓	X ↑
Y ↑	Z ↓	AA ↑	BB ↓

PLACEMENT DIAGRAM

 ↑   Arrow indicates
leaf direction    ↓

NAVAJO BLANKET

A knitted afghan by Blanche E. Rydel of Grand Rapids, Michigan

Proving how successfully other techniques can be adapted to knitting, this unusual work interprets Indian symbols taken from woven shawls and blankets dating back to around 1880.

about Blanche E. Rydel

When Blanche Rydel promised to replace an afghan she had made for her brother and sister-in-law (it was one of many prized possessions that burned in a fire in their home), she wanted a design that would fit in with their new den, planned with an Indian theme in mind. "My husband Dennis and I spent an evening at the public library," she recalls, absorbed in the fascinating tribal heritage of the southwest Indians. Doing her knitting in panels, she juxtaposed several weaving design motifs — the rising or setting sun, a symbol of life; the thunderbird, symbol of courage and strength worn by men in battle; and the symbol of the stairway to heaven — to produce an afghan of singular beauty and appeal.

NOTE *Work back and forth in rows on circular needle.*

SIZE About 63″ x 66½″, plus fringe.

MATERIALS Knitting worsted: 16 ozs. cream (color C), 10 ozs. taupe (T), 4 ozs. moss green (M), 8 ozs. apple green (A), 2 ozs. yellow (Y), 3 ozs. orange (O), 3 ozs. pumpkin (P), 3 ozs. rust (R), 2 ozs. black (B), 8 ozs. sand (S), 2 ozs. wine (W), 1 oz. gold (G), 4 ozs. light gray (L) and 3 ozs. dark red (D); 36″ circular knitting needle size 8 (or English needle size 5) **or the size that will give you the correct gauge.**

GAUGE 4 sts = 1″; 6 rows = 1″.

Working with pull balls See Knitting with Pull Balls, page 255. Wind yarn into pull balls as needed in colors specified, rewinding as necessary. When changing colors, twist yarn by bringing new color under yarn you have been working with to avoid holes in work. Attach another pull ball for each color change. Never carry any color yarn across back of work (except for C when working Chart 1). Break off pull ball when color area has been completed, leaving 5″ end to weave into wrong side of work.

AFGHAN Starting at one end with color T, cast on 250 sts. Work in stockinette st throughout as follows: Work 8 rows T.

Panel 1 Following Chart 1, work from W to X once, from X to Y 9 times and from Y to Z once on right-side rows and from Z to Y once, from Y to X 9 times and from X to W once on wrong-side rows until all 29 rows of chart have been completed. Work 10 rows T, dec 2 sts on last row (248 sts).

Each square = one stitch

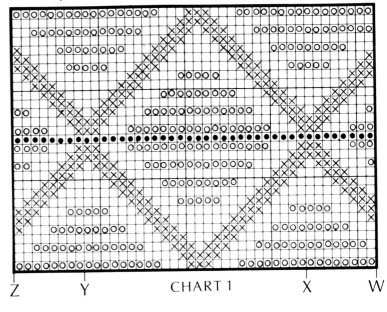

Z   Y   CHART 1   X   W

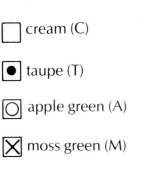

☐ cream (C)

⬤ taupe (T)

◯ apple green (A)

☒ moss green (M)

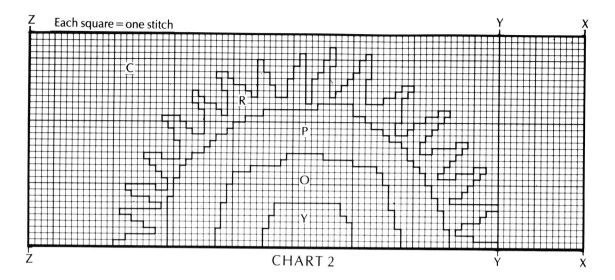

Panel 2 Following Chart 2, work from X to Y once and from Y to Z 3 times on right-side rows, and from Z to Y 3 times and from Y to X once on wrong-side rows, until all 34 rows of chart have been completed. Work 12 rows T, inc 3 sts on last row (251 sts).

Panel 3 Following Chart 3, work from X to Y once and from Y to Z 4 times on right-side rows, and from Z to Y 4 times and from Y to X once on wrong-side rows, until all 58 rows of chart have been completed. Work 14 rows T, dec 1 st on last row (250 sts).

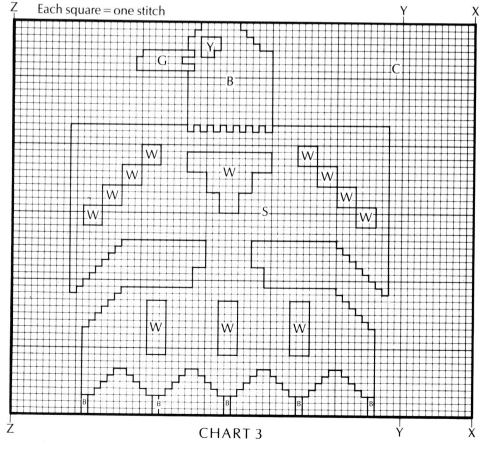

Panel 4 Following Chart 4, work from X to Y once and from Y to Z 3 times on right-side rows, and from Z to Y 3 times and from Y to X once on wrong-side rows, until all 68 rows of chart have been completed. Work 14 rows T, inc 1 st on last row (251 sts).

Work Panel 3, holding Chart 3 upside-down, working from Z to Y 4 times and Y to X once on right-side rows, and from X to Y once and Y to Z 4 times on wrong-side rows. Work 12 rows T, dec 3 sts on last row (248 sts).

Work Panel 2, holding Chart 2 upside-down, working from Z to Y 3 times and Y to X once on right-side rows, and from X to Y once and Y to Z 3 times on wrong-side rows. Work 10 rows T, inc 2 sts on last row (250 sts). Work Panel 1. Work 8 rows T. Bind off.

FINISHING With right side facing you, using crochet hook, work 1 row sc along each side edge of afghan, using C or T as needed to match colors.

Fringe Work tassel in every other stitch along each of the 2 ends (short sides) as follows: **Tassel** Cut six 7″ strands T. Holding strands together, fold in half to form loop. Insert crochet hook from wrong side through stitch and pull loop through work. Insert ends through loop and pull loop tight.

Each square = one stitch

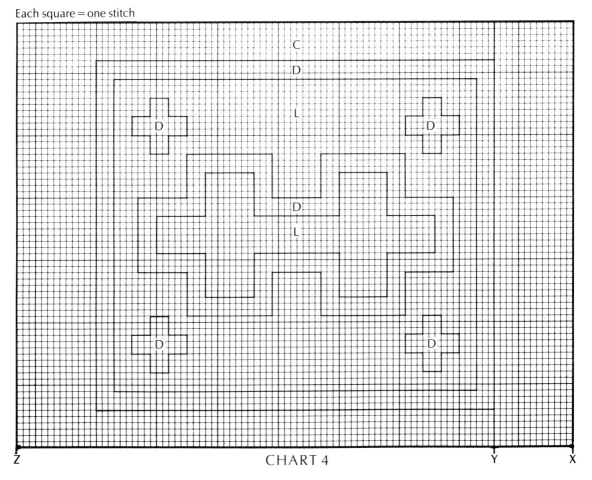

Z   CHART 4   Y   X

RAINBOW

A knitted afghan by Kiyoko Tatsui of Santa Ana, California

Brilliant bands meet to become bold chevrons in a rainbow of colors that vibrate and change right before your eyes.

*about
Kiyoko Tatsui*

Kiyoko Tatsui's subtle integration of technique and color tone creates an extraordinary knitted design — the ultimate contemporary interpretation of the conventional term "afghan." Going back and forth in rows on a circular needle, she used yarn bobbins in a spectrum of colors from violet to blue, green to yellow and orange to red, working them simultaneously across each row and watching them turn magically into chevrons as the work progressed.

NOTE *Afghan is worked back and forth in rows on circular needle. Wind 4 balls of each color, rewinding bobbins or pull balls as necessary (see Knitting with Pull Balls, page 255). Attach ball where specified or wherever you need one to work separate stripes. When changing colors, twist yarns by bringing new color under old to avoid holes in work. Break off ball when color area has been completed, leaving 5" end to weave into wrong side of work.*

SIZE About 63" x 80".

MATERIALS Knitting worsted: 6 ozs. white (color W), 4 ozs. each of violet (V), dark blue (DB), medium blue (MB), dark green (DG), medium green (MG), light yellow (LY), medium yellow (MY), orange (O) and red (R); 36" circular knitting needle size 9 (or English size 4) **or the size that will give you the correct gauge**.

GAUGE 7 sts = 2"; 5 rows = 1".

AFGHAN Starting at one end with W, cast on 220 sts. (Cast-on edge is top edge of afghan in photo.) Work in garter st (k every row) for 10 rows (border). **To establish rainbow design: 1st row** (right side): K 11 W (side border); k 11 V, 11 DB, 11 MB, 11 DG, 11 MG, 11 LY, 11 MY, 11 O, 22 R, 11 O, 11 MY, 11 LY, 11 MG, 11 DG, 11 MB, 11 DB, 11 V, 11 W (side border). **2nd and all even-numbered rows** K 11 W (border), p to last 11 sts in colors as established; k 11 W (border). **3rd and 4th rows** Repeat 1st and 2nd rows.

5th row K 11 W; attach DB and k in front of next st; with V, k in back of same st, k 9, sl next st as if to k, k 1, psso; k 10 DB, 11 MB, 11 DG, 11 MG, 11 LY, 11 MY, 11 O, 22 R, 11 O, 11 MY, 11 LY, 11 MG, 11 DG, 11 MB, 10 DB; with V, k 2 tog, k 9, k in front of next st; attach DB and k in back of same st; k 11 W.

7th row K 11 W; with DB, inc in next st; with V, k 10, sl 1, k 1, psso; k 9 DB, 11 MB, 11 DG, 11 MG, 11 LY, 11 MY, 11 O, 22 R, 11 O, 11 MY, 11 LY, 11 MG, 11 DG, 11 MB, 9 DB; with V, k 2 tog, k 10; with DB, inc in next st; k 11 W.

9th row K 11 W; with DB, inc in next st, k 1; with V, k 10, sl 1, k 1, psso; k 8 DB, 11 MB, 11 DG, 11 MG, 11 LY, 11 MY, 11 O, 22 R, 11 O, 11 MY, 11 LY, 11 MG, 11 DG, 11 MB, 8 DB; with V, k 2 tog, k 10; with DB, k1, inc in next st; k 11 W.

11th row K 11 W; with DB, inc in next st, k 2; with V, k 10, sl 1, k 1, psso; k 7 DB, 11 MB, 11 DG, 11 MG, 11 LY, 11 MY, 11 O, 22 R, 11 O, 11 MY, 11 LY, 11 MG, 11 DG, 11 MB, 7 DB; with V, k 2 tog, k 10; with DB, k 2, inc in next st; k 11 W.

13th row K 11 W; with DB, inc in next st, k 3; with V, k 10, sl 1, k 1, psso; k 6 DB, 11 MB, 11 DG, 11 MG, 11 LY, 11 MY, 11 O, 22 R, 11 O, 11 MY, 11 LY, 11 MG, 11 DG, 11 MB, 6 DB; with V, k 2 tog, k 10; with DB, k 3, inc in next st; k 11 W.

Continue in this manner, working W border sts in garter st and center sts in stockinette st and working inc inside border

edges and dec inside V stripes, until there are 11 DB sts inside each border, ending with an even-numbered (wrong-side) row.

27th row K 11 W; attach MB and k in front of next st; with DB, k in back of same st, k 10; with V, k 10, sl 1, k 1, psso; work across in colors as established to 1 st before next V stripe; with V, k 2 tog, k 10; with DB, k 10, k in front of next st; attach MB and k in back of same st; k 11 W.

29th row K 11 W; with MB, inc in next st; k 11 DB; with V, k 10, sl 1, k 1, psso; work in colors as established to 1 st before next V stripe; with V, k 2 tog, k 10; k 11 DB; with MB, inc in next st; k 11 W.

31st row K 11 W; with MB, inc in next st, k 1; k 11 DB; with V, k 10, sl 1, k 1, psso; work to 1 st before next V stripe; with V, k 2 tog, k 10; k 11 DB; with MB, k 1, inc in next st; k 11 W.

Continue in this manner, working W border sts in garter st, inc 1 st inside each border edge and dec 1 st inside each V stripe and work other colors as established, until there are 11 MB sts inside each border, ending with an even-numbered (wrong-side) row.

49th row K 11 W; attach DG and k in front of next st; with MB, k in back of same st, k 10; k 11 DB; with V, k 10, sl 1, k 1, psso; work to 1 st before V stripe; with V, k 2 tog, k 10; k11 DB; with MB, k 10, k in front of next st; attach DG and k in back of same st; k 11 W.

51st row K 11 W; with DG, inc in next st, k 11 MB, k 11 DB; with V, k 10, sl 1, k 1, psso; work to 1 st before V stripe; with V, k 2 tog, k 10; k 11 DB, k 11 MB; with DG, inc in next st; k 11 W.

Continuing as before, when there are 11 sts in color inside borders, attach new color on right-side row in the following color sequence: MG, LY, MY, O, R, V, DB, MB, DG, MG, LY, MY, O and R. At same time, whenever 2 diagonal stripes meet at center, break off color beneath and work at center with diagonal stripe color only, working dec with each succeeding color, until next diagonal stripe meets at center.

When color sequence is completed, work 2 rows in colors as established. Then, with W only, work 10 rows in garter st (border). Bind off.

SEA AND SHELLS

A knitted bedspread by Barbara Boulton of Ft. Myers, Florida

A beachcomber's delight — an afghan picturing that peaceful place where the ocean meets the shore, offering up treasures from the sea.

about Barbara Boulton

"Sanibel and shells have been my first love," writes Barbara Boulton from her needlework shop on Sanibel Island, off Florida's gulf coast. "On a clear day, there is nothing better than walking on the beach, searching for shells that are freshly washed in by the turquoise water." Since she has very little leisure time between running the business, conducting needlework classes and teaching high school, Barbara chose to make something for the contest that could be knitted quickly. Using extra-large needles, and two strands of yarn together for textural interest, she knitted her queen-sized spread in two weeks, working only in the evenings. "Designing the shells and putting them on in duplicate stitch was fun," says Barbara. "It only took me a week to stitch the shells."

NOTE *To wind and attach yarn pull balls, see Knitting with Pull Balls, page 255.*

SIZE About 63″ x 90″, plus 7″ fringe all around.

MATERIALS Knitting worsted: 16 ozs. blue and green ombré (color A), 12 ozs. light tan (B); Bernat Cloudspun: 10 (1¾-oz.) skeins baby blue (C), 6 skeins light tan (D); heavy-weight craft yarn or Bernat Big Berella, 1 (4-oz.) skein each of white (E) and brown (F); 1 pair size 15 knitting needles **or the size that will give you the correct gauge;** aluminum crochet hook size K (or international size 7.00 mm); large-eyed yarn needle for embroidery.

GAUGE 2 sts = 1″; 7 rows = 3″.

AFGHAN Working with one strand each of colors A and C held together, cast on 126 sts. Work in stockinette st for 45″, ending with a p row. Now work Chart 1, starting with the 3rd row of chart, working from X to Y as follows: K 4 with A and C (sea); attach a ball each of B and D, k 3 with one strand each of B and D (sand); attach another ball each of A and C, k to end with A and C (sea). Continuing, with 4th row of chart, work from Y to X on p rows and from X to Y on k rows, and up to Z in length, adding new balls of yarn to work each new section of sea and sand, and breaking off old balls of yarns as each sea section is completed. Continue with one ball each of B and D until afghan measures 63″ from beg. Bind off all sts.

Each square = one stitch

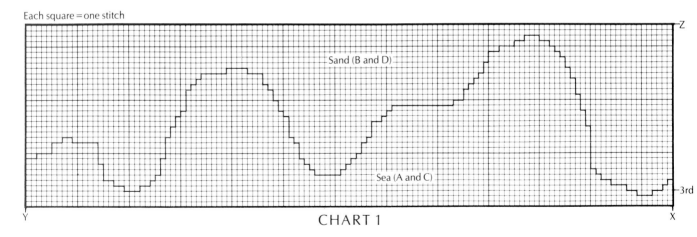

CHART 1

FINISHING Following Chart 2 for placement, embroider shells onto sand section using duplicate stitch (see directions and diagram, page 254). With crochet hook, A and C yarn and right side of work facing you, loosely work a row of sl sts (see page 248) along edges where sand and sea sections meet, following curves and covering jagged line where colors change. **Fringe** For each fringe, cut four 15″ strands of color A for sea section, of B for sand section. Fold strands in half; with crochet hook, draw folded end through edge st from front to back; draw cut ends through loop and draw tightly to knot. Make fringe in each st across top and bottom and in every other row along side edges of afghan, using A for sea section of afghan, B for sand section.

Color Key

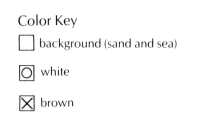

☐ background (sand and sea)

|O| white

|X| brown

Each square = one stitch

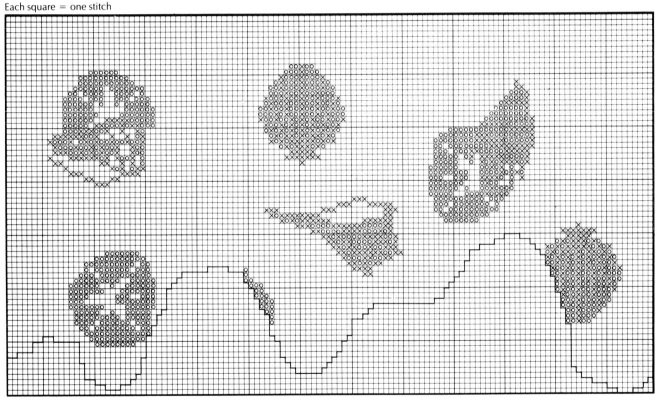

CHART 2

PART 4 General Directions

Patchwork or Piecework

QUILT TOP Use closely woven fabrics with soft textures. Calico, percale and muslin are good washable choices; be sure fabrics to be laundered are colorfast and preshrunk. Do not combine worn with new fabrics.

MATERIALS To estimate the quantity of materials needed, first decide on the amount of each color required for the individual block or unit. Multiply the results by the number of blocks or units in the quilt you are making. It is wise to have enough material to allow for possible waste in cutting.

Interlining Use cotton or polyester quilt batts. Polyester gives extra puffiness, as does a double thickness of cotton batting.

Backing May be the same fabric as the quilt top, joined in the same way. Or use a good grade of sheeting, which comes as wide as 90″, or use regular 36″-wide muslin and join strips to achieve the proper size. A muslin backing is easier to quilt than percale. Backing should be preshrunk.

PREPARING AND CUTTING PATTERNS
To enlarge patterns, see page 255. Trace pattern pieces onto tracing paper and then cut permanent pieces from thin cardboard, fine sandpaper, or blotters (use sandpaper rough side down when tracing on fabric and it will not slip). Lightweight linoleum can also be used to make patterns. Replace patterns from time to time as edges wear.

Place patterns on wrong side of fabric (or as directed), allowing at least ½″ between shapes. Pencil around patterns, being careful not to puncture, pull or stretch fabric. Pencil line will serve as sewing line. Cut out, allowing ¼″ all around outside from pencil line (for seams or turning). Separate patches by size and shape.

PIECING Assemble all the pieces for one unit or block of quilt. If the pattern is very intricate, pin or baste related pieces together. With right sides facing, join pieces with a small running or backstitch, following pencil line exactly. Clip seams of curved pieces after sewing.

SETTING Setting is the process of assembling the blocks or units of a quilt top and adding any strips or borders. Join blocks or units from the center out to insure smooth, unwarped results. Press all seams. It is best to press both seam edges to one side instead of pressing them open.

QUILTING DESIGNS You can quilt a top or leave it plain as you prefer. If you decide to quilt the top, mark it for quilting designs when it is completed.

Appliqué

Appliqué is the sewing down of pieces on a background. To enlarge patterns, should this be needed, see page 255.

MATERIALS Fabrics for appliqué should be compatible with the fabric to which they are to be applied. If you want the quilt to be washable, both should be colorfast and preshrunk. It is not wise to combine worn and new fabrics.

CUTTING Cut actual-size pattern pieces, as directed for patchwork, from thin cardboard, fine sandpaper, or blotters. (Use sandpaper rough side down so fabric will not slip.) Replace patterns as the edges wear. Place patterns on wrong side of fabric and pencil around them, allowing at least ½″ between pieces. Be careful not to puncture, pull or stretch fabric.

NOTE *In cutting pieces for appliqué, you may prefer, or need, to have the pencil line on the right side of the fabric.*

When patterns are traced, cut them out, allow-

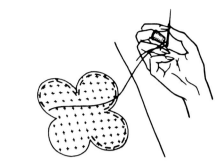

ing ¼″ seam or turning allowance all around. Separate the pieces according to shape and color. A good way of doing this is to stack all identical motifs in one pile and run a thread through the middle, leaving the knot under the pile. Then lift motifs from the top as needed.

The neatest way of appliquéing one material to another is to turn the seam allowance back over the pattern shape and press (see illustrations). Slash edges on curves to make them lie flat. To be sure of accurate placement, you can trace around your pattern on the foundation fabric. Then follow these lines when basting appliqué pieces in place. This is especially helpful if a design is intricate. Position the appliqué, with edges turned under, on your foundation and baste in place.

SETTING See Patchwork.

SEWING Many different stitches can be used to appliqué pieces. The one used most often is a regular hemming stitch. You can also use a slip-stitch or even a buttonhole stitch. The main thing is to make neat, even stitches. Use thread in a color that matches the piece you are sewing. Sometimes decorative stitches are worked on edges after appliqué is completed. Feather stitch or blanket stitch makes a pretty edge. When bias strips are used on a curved line, baste the inside edge first. The material can then be stretched until it lies flat along the outer edge.

If you are an experienced sewer or after you have practiced awhile, you can use shortcuts such as pressing under seam allowance with your thumb and forefinger or simply pinning your appliqué in place and turning under the seam allowance as you sew. It is when you use such a shortcut method to appliqué that the pencil lines on the right side of the piece are helpful.

To enrich certain areas of design, appliqué is sometimes padded. To do this, leave a small section open when sewing; stuff cotton batting in opening, pushing it under the appliqué piece with a knitting needle until it is firm and even; then finish sewing the piece down.

Quilting

NOTE *These directions are for quilting coverlets. Many quilting designs may also be used on patchwork and appliqué coverlets for quilted borders and backgrounds.*

MATERIALS A special quilting thread is generally used for cotton, linen or wool quilts because it is extra-strong and has a smooth finish that makes it glide easily through layers of material. If that is not available, mercerized thread between Nos. 50 and 70 should be used. If your coverlet is of silk or rayon, silk thread should be used. Generally the thread should be the same color as the background fabric.

QUILT TOP Fine quilting deserves the very best materials available, whether cotton, silk, rayon, linen or wool. Fabrics should be firmly woven, soft in texture, and of good quality. If you want to be able to wash your coverlet, the fabric should be preshrunk and, if colored, colorfast to laundering. If there is any doubt, wash a small sample

before starting the quilt. In the cotton family, calico, percale, muslin or cotton satin may be used. For a more luxurious coverlet, silks, rayons, linens or wools are possibilities.

QUILTING If you are working out your own quilt, after the top is assembled, plan placement of quilting designs. Using graph paper and having each square equal one square inch of your coverlet, make an overall plan. Sketch the quilting patterns that you want to use—borders, center and other design areas—in scale on the plan. This will give you an idea of how your arrangement of patterns will look on your finished quilt and whether they are in proportion. When designs are decided upon, using pins or basting thread, outline the areas on the quilt that correspond to those sketched on the plan. This is the time to chart mathematically the placement of border repeats. It is generally easier to start a border design at the center of each edge and work repeats toward corners so that the design may be adjusted to make its parts meet attractively.

TRANSFERRING QUILTING PATTERNS To enlarge patterns, see page 255. If you use washable fabrics, you can trace full-size designs with tracing wheel and dressmaker's carbon paper. Or you can transfer markings by a traditional method. First perforate the full-size designs you wish to use with a tracing wheel, a large pin or needle, or stitch along lines on a sewing machine with needle unthreaded. Then, following your quilting plan, place quilt top on a firm surface and pin perforated pattern securely in position. Cover a small pad of cotton with soft cloth. Dip in cinnamon, cocoa, or a mixture of 1 teaspoonful of powdered ultramarine (available from drugstores) to 4 teaspoonfuls of cornstarch. Pat powder over perforations to distribute evenly, then rub lightly with scrubbing motion to work it through perforations, *making certain that neither fabric nor pattern moves.* Carefully remove pattern and blow off excess powder, then go over design lightly with a soft lead pencil. Background designs are generally marked after special designs are quilted and with the quilt still in the frame.

QUILTING FRAME Large pieces such as quilts require a frame long enough to enclose the entire piece or a convenient working section; a small item can be worked with an ordinary embroidery hoop. Either may be purchased through specialized mail-order houses or from needlework shops or departments. If you wish, you can make your own frame. Such a frame consists of four wooden strips, about 1″ x 2″ thick and wide, and long enough together to enclose the entire quilt, or, if that is not convenient, one half or one quarter of the quilt, when strips are joined. Fasten strips where they cross at corners with clamps. Rest frame on supports such as chair backs, which will bring it almost to chest height for working.

ASSEMBLING QUILT Thumbtack a 2″ strip of firm muslin securely along top edge of frame. Pin or baste your quilt lining to this securely, stretching it smooth and taut. Spread quilt batt over lining. Over all place the quilt top. Smooth layers and baste together diagonally from center to all four corners of quilt (or quilt section) and around outer edges, avoiding either unnecessary fullness or extreme tightness.

QUILTING STITCH Many old counterpanes were quilted with backstitch or chain stitch, but today's quilting patterns usually use a simple running stitch. A beginner in quilting should try a small practice piece, because the thickness of the layers and the puffiness of the filling often make it difficult for the inexperienced to make short, even stitches at first. One method is to hold the needle nearly horizontal, rather than on a slant as you do for ordinary sewing, and take several stitches before drawing the needle away from the quilt. Another method that is slower but unfailingly accurate is to make the stitch in two separate movements: The left hand is placed under the frame to receive the needle, which is pushed vertically downward from the top. Then, with the left hand, the needle is pushed upward to complete the stitch. This method is generally used when the quilts are of heavy material or if the filling is thick. To begin quilting, thread needle, make a knot at the end of the thread and bring needle through to top of quilt at design starting point. Pull gently but firmly until knot pulls through backing into batting. Fasten thread with a backstitch and run end of thread into batting.

RAISED QUILTING

These are techniques, always done before other quilting, by which designs or design parts are stuffed to give them a puffed or dimensional look. The filling may be cotton batting or absorbent cotton (padded quilting) or a cord or yarn filler (trapunto, or corded quilting). Since either filling is inserted at the back (underside) of the quilt top, it is necessary to baste an interlining (such as good-quality cheesecloth or muslin) underneath the design parts to be stuffed before attaching the backing. Transfer the affected quilting designs to this fabric interlining. With interlining facing up, quilt design through it and top fabric. To pad a design carefully part threads of interlining with bodkin or knitting needle and insert small bits of cotton padding between the two layers of fabric into each small area.

Trapunto, or corded quilting, applies to linear designs and outlines. Stems and vines are typical candidates for this kind of "raising." To work the technique, two closely parallel lines of quilting are necessary. Upholstery cording or cotton rug yarn is then run through the casing formed by the quilting lines. At deep curves and sharp turns, the needle must be brought through interlining at curve or turn and then inserted again, leaving a small loop of yarn. Cording should never be drawn through to top of quilt.

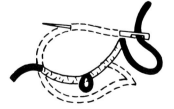

Stuff designs evenly and firmly so they will stand in relief on quilt top. After stuffing or/and cording are completed (they are often used together), transfer other quilting patterns to top fabric. Assemble quilt and backing, place in frame, and quilt remainder as usual.

BACKGROUND QUILTING When motifs and border are completed and while quilt is still on frame, pencil in background pattern. Use a yardstick for straight lines and cups, saucers, egg cups, even fifty-cent pieces for circular designs. Diagonal lines have always been one of the most popular of backgrounds. They are generally $1/4''$ to $3/4''$ apart. Other very effective ruled patterns are squares, diamonds, and diagonal plaids. Egg cups or fifty-cent pieces are fine guides for drawing shell or cloud backgrounds. Interlocking circles, however, are more effective when larger circular objects are used, such as saucers or bread-and-butter plates.

MACHINE QUILTING Although classic quilting is considered a handcraft, it may be done by sewing machine, preferably on small projects or larger ones that can be worked in parts. A bed-size quilt is very difficult to maneuver under the needle — and under the arm — of a sewing machine.

Straight quilting lines and simple designs are most adaptable to machine work. For this it is essential that the quilt top, interlining and backing be basted together most securely. Basting lines should be not more than $2''$ apart to prevent shifting of fabric during stitching.

BINDING QUILTS When quilting is completed, remove the quilt from the frame and trim edges, making sure to clip off any batting that extends beyond the quilt top. Bind edges with double-fold bias tape or matching fabric cut in bias strips and joined to required length.

Embroidery Stitches

BACKSTITCH

For lines and outlines, and as a foundation for other stitches. Work from right to left. Bring needle up a short distance from start of line to be covered; insert it at start of line. Bring out an equal distance ahead along line; draw needle through.

BASKET FILLING STITCH

Alternate four vertical with four horizontal satin stitches.

BASKET STITCH

For solid lines and borders. Work from top to bottom. Bring needle up on left line; insert it lower down on right line and bring out directly opposite on left line. Then insert needle on right line above stitch just made; bring out on left just below point where thread first emerged. Insert needle on right line below lowest stitch there and bring out exactly opposite. Take a stitch as shown, working in same holes into which other stitches were worked. Repeat last two steps. The needle takes a step forward and backward alternately.

BLANKET STITCH

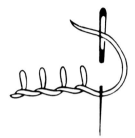

For covering a turned-over edge, for outlining or, when worked in a circle, to form flowers. Work from left to right. Bring needle up on lower line. Hold thread down with left thumb. Insert needle a little to the right of starting point on upper line; bring out directly below on bottom line; draw needle through over loop of thread.

BRAID STITCH

For borders. Work from right to left. Bring needle up on lower line. Make a loop of thread as shown in diagram; hold down with thumb; insert needle through loop and into fabric at top of line; bring out on lower line. Pull loop on needle tight; draw through over thread.

CHAIN STITCH

For lines and outlines. Worked in close rows, it is used as a filling stitch. Bring needle to right side of fabric. Hold thread down with thumb. Insert needle as close as possible to spot where thread emerges, bring out a short distance below. Draw needle through over loop.

CHAIN STITCH – OPEN

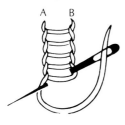

For borders, wide lines and casings. Work from top to bottom. Bring needle out at A. Hold thread down with thumb; insert needle at B, bring out a little below A, draw thread through over working thread. Leave loop just formed a little loose; the next stitch is inserted in it. Work subsequent stitches as shown in diagram.

CHAIN STITCH – TWISTED

For lines and borders. Work from top to bottom. Work as chain stitch but take a slanting stitch as shown and do not work back into previous stitch.

CLOUD FILLING STITCH

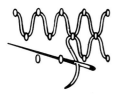

For filling. Make a foundation of tiny stitches as shown. Then lace through these stitches, first those on top, then those on bottom, to end of row. On next row, lace stitches so loops meet under the same stitch as shown.

CORAL STITCH

For lines, outlines and filling. Work from right to left. Bring thread up at start of line to be covered. Hold down with thumb, then make a tiny slanting stitch along line and draw needle through over thread as shown.

COUCHING STITCH

For outlines, lines and borders. Place one or more threads along line to be covered; hold down with thumb. With another thread, work small even stitches over the line of threads to hold them in place. Both couching and laid yarn can be the same color, or they can contrast. Laid yarn can also be an entirely different material, such as cord or metallic yarn.

COUCHING STITCH – BOKHARA

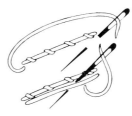

For filling. Worked same as couching but the same thread is used for both the ground and the tying-down stitches. Carry thread across space to be filled from left to right; then work back as shown, making small slanting stitches at even intervals over this thread. The tying-down stitches should be close together and pulled tight.

CRETAN STITCH – OPEN

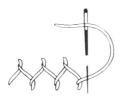

For lines, borders or filling. Work from left to right. Bring needle up on lower line. Make a small vertical stitch on top line as shown. Then, with needle pointing up, make a similar stitch on lower line.

CROSS-STITCH

Usually worked with transfers or on fabric where threads can be counted, since crosses should be even. Make a row of slanting stitches over an equal number of threads of fabric. This forms a row of the first half of each cross. Work back over these stitches, completing the second half, as shown. You can work cross-stitches individually and in any direction, but they must all be crossed in the same direction.

FEATHER STITCH

For lines, borders, outlines, fernlike leaves and light filling. Work from top to bottom. Bring needle up a little to left of line to be covered. Hold thread down with thumb; make a slanting stitch to the right and a little below this spot with needle pointing to the left; draw needle through over working thread. Carry thread to left side of line to be covered and make a similar stitch a little below this spot with needle pointing to the right; draw needle through over working thread.

FERN STITCH

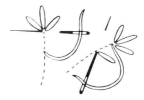

For leaf veins or fernlike leaves. Work three straight stitches all radiating from same center hole.

FISHBONE STITCH

For filling. Make a short stitch at top of area to be filled. Bring needle up on left margin; insert it a little below first stitch and just across center line; bring out on right margin. Make a similar stitch, inserting needle to left of center line and bringing it out at left margin. Each succeeding stitch should slant and cross at the center.

FRENCH KNOT

For flower center, light filling, and anywhere that the effect of a single dot is required. Bring needle up at point where knot is to be made. Wind thread two or three times around point of needle; insert in fabric as close as possible to spot where thread emerged (but not in exact spot) and pull to wrong side, holding twists in place.

HERRINGBONE STITCH

For borders, wide lines, and as a foundation for other stitches. Work from left to right. Bring needle up at A; insert at B, bring out at C; then insert at D, bring out at E, etc.

LAZY DAISY STITCH

For flowers and light filling. Bring thread up in center of "flower." Hold the thread down with thumb; insert needle close to or in exact spot where thread emerged and bring out desired distance below; draw through over working thread. Then tie down with a tiny stitch made over loop as shown. Make similar stitches to form a circle around same center point. Diagram shows them separated for clarity, but they can be made in same center hole.

LONG AND SHORT STITCH

For filling and shading. Work same as satin stitch (see below), but stagger long and short stitches over area to be covered. The irregular line formed by these stitches is especially good for shading.

LOOP STITCH

An improvised stitch made by looping thread or yarn over your thumb as you work outline stitch (see below), making loops on right side of work. Make a loop, then a small stitch in usual way to secure thread, then another loop, and so on.

OUTLINE STITCH

Also called stem or crewel stitch. For outlines, stems and any fine line. Work from left to right. Bring needle up at end of line to be covered. Insert needle a short distance to the right and bring out a little way to the left at a slight angle. Keep thread above needle.

ROMAN STITCH

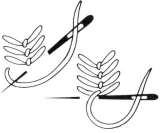

For borders or filling. Work from top to bottom. Bring needle up on left line; insert exactly opposite on right line; bring out in center. Then make a tiny stitch over this loop and bring needle out on left line (second step). Stitches can be made slightly curved as shown or perfectly straight.

RUNNING STITCH

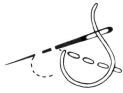

For outlines and foundations for other stitches; for filling when worked in close rows. Work from right to left as shown.

SATIN STITCH

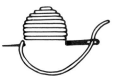

For filling where background fabric is to be covered completely. Bring needle up at one edge of area to be covered, insert needle at opposite edge and return to starting line by carrying it underneath fabric. Make stitches close enough together to cover background fabric completely. Satin stitches should not be so long that they look loose and untidy. You can divide large areas to be covered into small sections.

SHEAF FILLING STITCH

For filling. Make three vertical satin stitches. Then bring needle up beneath them at center and bring out at left side; wrap thread around center twice without picking up fabric and insert where thread emerged.

SPLIT STITCH

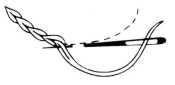

For outlines, stems and lines. When worked in close rows, it is used for filling, and by working rows in different colors, for shading. Work stitch like outline stitch (above) but with thread below the needle; then split working thread close to its base when you bring needle out.

STAR STITCH

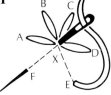

Bring needle up at A, down at X (center), up at B, down at X, up at C, down at X and so on to complete star.

VANDYKE STITCH

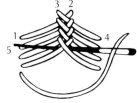

For borders and lines. Bring needle up at 1. Insert at 2 and bring out at 3. Then insert at 4 and bring out at 5. For next stitch, insert needle under center-crossed stitches and, without picking up fabric, draw needle through. Insert needle in right margin below last stitch, bring out directly below on left.

Crochet

HOOKS Crochet hooks come in a wide range of sizes and lengths and are made of various materials. Steel crochet hooks are generally used for cotton thread and come in sizes 00, the largest, through 16, the smallest. Aluminum and plastic hooks, used for wool yarn and cotton thread, usually come in sizes A through K, size A being the smallest. Afghan hooks are manufactured especially for afghan stitch. They are about the length of knitting needles, either 9″ or 14″ long, and come in the same sizes as other crochet hooks.

MATERIALS There are many variations in the weight, twist, finish and color of crochet threads. The fine mercerized cotton threads are effective for delicate designs used in edgings, doilies and tablecloths; wool yarns are best for afghans, baby garments, sweaters, and other wearing apparel. The heaviest cotton, wool, and jute yarns are used for rugs. Buy all the thread or yarn you will need at one time to be sure of having the same dye lot. Slight variations in weight and color can ruin the appearance of your work.

GAUGE It is important that you crochet to the gauge specified so that your finished article will be the correct size. Gauge means the number of stitches and rows that make a 1″ square. Make a practice piece at least 2″ square, using the hook and materials specified in the directions. With a ruler, measure the number of stitches you have to 1″ in your test piece.

If your stitches do not correspond to the gauge given, experiment with a different-size hook. If you have more stitches than specified to the inch, use a larger hook; if you have fewer stitches, use a smaller hook. Keep changing the hook size until your gauge is the same as that specified.

ABBREVIATIONS AND TERMS

beg . . . . beginning
b . . . . bobble
bl . . . . block
ch . . . . chain
cl . . . . cluster
dc . . . . double crochet
dec . . . . decrease
d tr . . . . double treble
h dc . . . . half double crochet
inc . . . . increase
lp . . . . .loop
O . . . . thread over
pc . . . . popcorn
rnd .round
sc . . . . single crochet
sk . . . . .skip
sl . . . . slip
sl st . . . . slip stitch
sp . . . . space
st . . . . stitch
sts .stitches
tog . . . . together
tr . . . . .treble
tr tr . . . . triple treble
yo . . . . yarn over

* Asterisk means repeat the instructions following the asterisk as many times as specified, in addition to the first time.

[ ] *Brackets* are used to designate changes in size when directions are given, as they often are, for more than one size. The figure preceding the brackets refers to the smallest size.

Even When directions say "work even," this means to continue working without increasing or decreasing, following pattern as established.

Multiple of stitches A pattern often requires an exact number of stitches to be worked correctly. When directions say "multiple of," it means the number of stitches must be divisible by this number. For example: (Multiple of 6) would be 12, 18, 24, etc.; (multiple of 6 plus 3) would be 15, 21, 27, etc.

( ) *Parentheses* mean repeat instructions in parentheses as many times as specified. For example: "(Ch 5, sc in next sc) 5 times" means to do all that is specified in parentheses a total of 5 times.

TO BEGIN CROCHET As a general rule, make a practice piece of each new stitch, working until you can do it well and comfortably.

The first loop

1. Make a loop at the end of the thread and hold loop in place with thumb and forefinger of left hand. At left is short end of thread; at right is the long or working thread.

2. With right hand, grasp the crochet hook as you would a pencil and put hook through loop, catch working thread and draw it through.

3. Pull short end and working thread in opposite directions to bring loop close around the end of hook.

To hold thread

1. Measure down working thread about 4″ from loop on hook.

2. At this point, insert thread between ring finger and little finger of left hand.

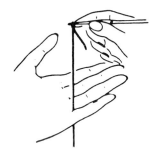

3. Weave thread toward back as shown: under little and ring fingers, over middle finger, and under forefinger toward you.

4. Grasp hook and loop with thumb and forefinger of left hand.

5. Gently pull working thread so that it is taut but not tight.

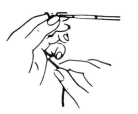

To hold hook

1. Hold hook as you would a pencil, except extend middle finger to rest near tip of hook.

2. To begin working, adjust fingers of left hand as in diagram.

The middle finger is bent so it can control the tension, while the ring and little fingers prevent the thread from moving too freely. As you practice, you will become accustomed to the correct tension. Now you are ready to begin the chain stitch.

CHAIN STITCH (ch)

1. Pass hook under thread and catch thread with hook. This is called thread over—O.

2. Draw thread through loop on hook. This makes one chain.

3. Repeat steps 1 and 2 until you have as many chain stitches as you need. One loop always remains on hook. Keep thumb and forefinger of your left hand near stitch on which you are working. Practice until chains are uniform.

SINGLE CROCHET (sc)

Make a foundation chain of 20 stitches for practice piece.

1. Insert hook from the front under 2 top threads of 2nd chain from hook.

2. Thread over hook.

3. Draw through stitch. Two loops now on hook.

4. Thread over (*below left*). Draw through 2 loops on hook. One loop remains on hook. One single crochet completed (*below right*).

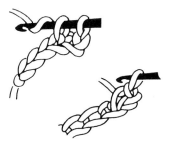

5. For next single crochet, insert hook under 2 top threads of next stitch. Repeat steps 2, 3 and 4. Make a single crochet in each chain.

6. At end of row, chain 1 (turning chain).

7. Turn work so reverse side is facing you.

8. Insert hook under 2 top threads of first single crochet. Repeat steps 2, 3, 4, 5, 6, and 7. Continue working single crochet in this manner until work is uniform and you feel familiar with the stitch. On last row, do not make a turning chain. Instead, clip thread about 3″ from work, bring loose end through the one remaining loop on hook, and pull tight.

Now you have completed your practice piece of single crochet.

NOTE *In all crochet, pick up the 2 top threads of every stitch unless otherwise specified. When only one thread is picked up, the effect is different.*

DOUBLE CROCHET (dc)

Make a foundation chain of 20 stitches for practice piece.

1. Thread over, insert hook under the 2 top threads of 4th chain from hook.

2. Thread over, draw through stitch. There are now 3 loops on hook.

3. Thread over (*see diagram*). Draw through 2 loops. Two loops remain on hook.

4. Thread over again.

Draw through the 2 remaining loops. One loop remains on hook. One double crochet now is completed.

5. For next double crochet, thread over, insert hook under the 2 top threads of next stitch and repeat steps 2, 3, and 4. Repeat until you have made a double crochet in each stitch.

6. At end of row, chain 3 and turn work.

7. On next row, thread over, skip first double crochet, insert hook under the 2 top threads of 2nd double crochet. Repeat steps 2, 3, 4, 5, 6, and 7.

8. Continue working double crochet in this manner until work is uniform and you feel familiar with the stitch. On last row, do not make a turning chain. Instead, clip thread about 3″ from work, bring loose end through the one remaining loop on hook, and pull tight.

HALF DOUBLE CROCHET (hdc)

To make half double crochet, repeat steps 1 and 2 under Double Crochet but insert hook in 3rd chain from hook. At this point there are 3 loops on hook. Then thread over and draw through all 3 loops at once.

Half double crochet is now completed. At end of row, chain 2 to turn.

TREBLE CROCHET (tr)

Make a foundation chain of 20 stitches for practice piece.

1. Thread over twice, insert hook under 2 top threads of 5th chain from hook.

2. Thread over and draw a loop through the chain. There are now 4 loops on hook.

3. Thread over again (*next diagram*). Draw through 2 loops on hook (3 loops remain on hook).

4. Thread over again (*next diagram*). Draw through 2 loops (2 loops remain on hook).

5. Thread over again.

Draw through 2 remaining loops (one loop remains on hook). One treble crochet is now completed. At end of row, chain 4 to turn. Continue making treble crochet in this manner until you are familiar with the stitch. Finish piece same as other pieces.

DOUBLE TREBLE (d tr)

Thread over hook 3 times, insert hook under 2 top threads of 6th chain from hook and draw a loop through the chain (5 loops on hook). Thread over and draw through 2 loops at a time 4 times. A double treble is now completed (*see diagram*). At end of row, chain 5 to turn.

TRIPLE TREBLE (tr tr)

Thread over hook 4 times, insert hook under 2 top threads of 7th chain from hook and draw a loop through the chain (6 loops on hook). Thread over and draw through 2 loops at a time 5 times. A triple treble is now completed (*see diagram*). At end of row, chain 6 to turn.

BASIC TECHNIQUES
To turn work

You will notice that stitches vary in length. Each uses a different number of chain stitches to turn at the end of a row. Below is a table showing the number of chain stitches required to make a turn for each stitch.

Single crochet (sc): ch 1
Half double crochet (hdc): ch 2
Double crochet (dc): ch 3
Treble crochet (tr): ch 4
Double treble (dtr): ch 5
Triple treble (trtr): ch 6

To decrease (dec) single crochet

1. Work one single crochet to point where 2 loops are on hook. Draw up a loop in next stitch.

2. Thread over, draw thread through 3 loops at one time. One decrease made.

To decrease (dec) double crochet

1. Work one double crochet to point where 2 loops are on hook. Begin another double crochet in next stitch and work until 4 loops are on hook.

2. Thread over, draw through 2 loops.

3. Thread over, draw through 3 loops (*see diagram*). One decrease made.

To increase (inc)

When directions call for an increase, work 2 stitches in one stitch. This forms one extra stitch.

SLIP STITCH (sl st)

Make a foundation chain of 20 stitches for practice piece. Insert hook under top thread of 2nd chain from hook, thread over. With one motion draw through stitch and loop on hook. Insert hook under top thread of next chain, then thread over and draw through stitch and loop on hook.

Repeat until you have made a slip stitch in each chain. A chain with slip stitch is often used for ties on baby garments. Rows of slip stitch worked in the back loop of each stitch produce a ribbed effect.

Slip stitch for joining

When directions say "join," always use a slip stitch.

1. Insert hook through the 2 top threads of stitch.

2. Thread over and with one motion draw through stitch and loop on hook.

Working around the post

The "post" or "bar" is the vertical or upright portion of a stitch. When directions say to make a stitch around the post or bar of a stitch in a previous row, insert the hook *around* stitch instead of in top of stitch. See diagram below for placement of hook.

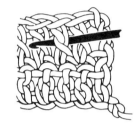

AFGHAN STITCH

This stitch requires a long hook to hold a number of stitches at one time. Though as the name of the stitch implies it is used primarily for afghans, it is equally effective for crocheting sweaters, scarves, and other articles. Make a foundation chain of 20 stitches for practice piece.

1. Insert hook under 2 top threads of 2nd chain from hook; thread over and draw a loop through chain.

2. Retaining all loops on hook, draw up a loop in each remaining chain.

3. When all loops are one hook, thread over, draw through one loop; thread over, draw through 2 loops.

4. Thread over, draw through next 2 loops (*as in next diagram*). Repeat this sequence across row. Loop remaining on hook at end of row always counts as first stitch of next row. Do not turn.

5. To begin 2nd and succeeding rows, insert hook in the front thread of the 2nd vertical bar.

6. Draw up a loop. Retaining all loops on hook, draw up a loop in the front thread of each vertical bar across to within last vertical bar.

Insert hook in front thread of last vertical bar and the stitch directly behind it and draw up a loop. This gives a firm edge to this side.

7. Work off loops as in first row, drawing through one loop first and then through 2 loops progressively across row. On last row of work, make a slip stitch in each vertical bar to keep edge from curling.

To increase afghan stitch To increase one stitch, draw up a loop in chain between vertical bars.

To decrease afghan stitch To decrease one stitch, insert hook under 2 vertical bars and draw up one loop.

Cross-stitch over afghan stitch Because afghan stitch forms almost perfect squares, when an article is completed it is often embroidered with cross-stitch.

BASIC SHELL STITCH

This is the first and simplest of the many varieties of shell stitch. Once you have learned this basic stitch, you'll find directions for the others easy to follow. Make a foundation chain (multiple of 6 stitches plus 4) for practice piece.

1st row Work 2 dc in 4th ch from hook (half shell), skip 2 ch, 5 dc in next ch (shell made), skip 2 ch, sc in next ch. Repeat from * across, ending with 3 dc in last ch (another half shell). Ch 1, turn. **2nd row** Sc in first dc, * skip 2 dc, shell (5 dc) in next sc, skip 2 dc, sc in center dc of next shell. Repeat from * across, ending with sc in top of half shell. Ch 3, turn. **3rd row** Work 2 dc in first sc, * sc in center dc of next shell, shell in next sc. Repeat from * across, ending with 3 dc in last sc. Ch 1, turn. Repeat 2nd and 3rd rows for desired length.

FINISHING After you have completed an article, thread each loose end of thread or yarn in a needle and darn it through a solid part of the crochet to fasten it securely. Cut off remaining thread close to the work. Be sure starting ends are long enough to be fastened off.

LAUNDERING If your work has become soiled, wash it by hand before blocking. Launder cotton-thread work in thick suds of a mild soap and hot water; wash woolens in cold-water soap or mild soap and lukewarm water. Squeeze but do not wring the article. Rinse in lukewarm water several times until soap is thoroughly removed. Roll in a bath towel to absorb some of the moisture.

BLOCKING If an article is made up of several pieces, block them before sewing them together. If you have laundered your work, block it while still damp. Place article wrong side up on a flat, padded surface. Gently stretch and shape it to the desired measurements; pin to surface, using rust-

proof pins, preferably ballpoint. Press through a dry cloth with a hot iron. Do not slide the iron but move it lightly from place to place, being careful not to press the weight of the iron down hard on the article. Let dry thoroughly before unpinning. If you have not had to launder your work, pin the dry article on a padded surface; press through a damp cloth.

SEWING Pin together edges to be sewed; matching any pattern in rows or stitches. Thread needle with matching thread or yarn. To begin sewing, do not knot thread but take several over and over stitches, darning them, if possible, through a solid part of the crochet. Sew straight, even edges with a whip stitch, placing it at the edges of the work. Sew slanting or uneven edges, caused by increasing or decreasing, with a backstitch, placing it just inside edges. On woolen articles, leave stitches loose enough to match garment's elasticity.

Knitting

NEEDLES Knitting needles come in a wide range of sizes, types and lengths and are made of several different materials. Straight needles with single points are used when you work back and forth in rows. Circular needles are usually used when you work in rounds. They are also used when a straight needle is not long enough to hold a large number of stitches. Double-pointed needles come in sets of four. They are used for tubular garments, when you work in rounds or for turning cables. Large needles are used for heavy yarn and smaller needles for thinner yarn.

YARNS AND THREADS Many types of yarn and thread are used for knitting. They differ as to twist, size, texture and weight. The material specified in directions has always been chosen to suit the article that is being made. Only an expert knitter should attempt to substitute materials. Buy all the thread or yarn you need at one time to be sure of having the same dye lot. Slight variations in weight and color can ruin the appearance of your work.

ABBREVIATIONS AND TERMS

beg	beginning
dec	decrease
dp	double-pointed
inc	increase
k	knit
O	thread over
p	purl
psso	pass slipped stitch over
rnd	round
sl	slip
sl st	slip stitch
st	stitch
sts	stitches
tog	together
yo	yarn over

* *Asterisk* means repeat the instructions following the asterisk as many times as specified, in addition to the first time.

[ ] *Brackets* are used to designate change in size when directions are given, as they often are, for more than one size. The figure preceding the brackets refers to the smallest size.

Even When directions say ''work even,'' this means to continue working without increasing or decreasing, always keeping the pattern as it has been established.

Multiple of stitches A pattern often requires an exact number of stitches to be worked correctly. When directions say ''multiple of,'' it means the number of stitches must be divisible by this number. For example: (Multiple of 6) would be 12, 18, 24, etc.; (multiple of 6 plus 3) would be 15, 21, 27, etc.

( ) *Parentheses* mean repeat instruction in parentheses as many times as specified. For example:

"(K 3, p 2) 5 times" means to do all that is specified in parentheses 5 times in all.

Place a marker in work This term means to mark with a safety pin a certain point in the work itself to use as a guide in taking future measurements.

Place a marker on needle This term means to place a safety pin, paper clip, or bought plastic stitch marker on the needle between the stitches. It is slipped from one needle to the other to serve as a mark on following rows.

Slip a stitch When directions say "slip a stitch" or "sl 1," insert right needle in stitch to be slipped as if to purl and simply pass from left to right needle without working it.

GAUGE It is most important that you knit to the gauge specified so that your finished article will be the correct size. Gauge means the number of stitches that equal 1″ and the number of rows that equal 1″. Make a practice piece at least 4″ square, using the needles and yarn specified in the directions. With a ruler, measure the number of stitches you have to 1″ in both directions. If your stitches do not correspond to the gauge given, experiment with needles of a different size. If you have more stitches than specified to the inch, you should use larger needles. If you have fewer stitches to the inch, use smaller needles. Keep changing the needle size until your gauge is exactly the same as that specified.

TO BEGIN KNITTING For a practice piece, use knitting worsted and No. 6 needles.

To cast on Make a slip loop several inches from yarn end and insert point of needle through it (*see first diagram*). Tighten loop. Hold needle with

tightened loop in left hand. Hold second needle in right hand, with yarn in working position as shown in diagram below.

Insert point of right needle in loop on left needle from left to right. With index finger bring the yarn over the point of right needle as shown in next diagram.

Draw the yarn through the loop, as below.

Insert left needle through new loop (*next diagram*) and remove right needle. You now have 2 stitches cast on. You can make the 3rd and all succeeding stitches in the same way, or, for a

stronger edge, you can insert right needle between stitches just below left needle instead of through loops (*see below*).

Cast on 15 stitches for a practice swatch. You are now ready to begin knitting.

KNIT STITCH

Hold needle with cast-on stitches in left hand. Insert right needle in front of first stitch on left needle from left to right. With right hand, bring yarn under and over the point of right needle and draw the yarn through the stitch; slip the old stitch off the left needle. This completes first stitch of row. Repeat in each stitch until all stitches have

been knitted off left needle. Always push work along left needle so that stitch to be worked is near tip. When row is completed, you should have 15 stitches on the right needle just as you had on the left originally. Count stitches occasionally to make sure that you keep the same number. At the end of row, turn work so needle with stitches is in your left hand. Continue working rows in this manner until work is uniform and you feel familiar with the stitch. When you knit each stitch in each row in this way, it is called garter stitch.

To bind off You are now ready to finish off your practice piece. This process is called binding off. Loosely knit 2 stitches. With point of left needle, pick up first stitch and slide it over second; slip it off needle. * Knit next stitch and slip preceding one over it. Repeat from * across.

When you come to your last stitch, cut yarn about 3″ from the needle. Bring loose end through last stitch and pull tightly. Darn in end with tapestry needle so that it will not show.

PURL STITCH

You make this stitch with the yarn in front of work instead of back and insert needle in stitch from the right instead of left. The wrong side of a purl stitch is a knit stitch. The purl stitch is rarely used alone, so to practice the stitch it is best to proceed with stockinette stitch.

STOCKINETTE STITCH

Cast on 15 stitches for practice swatch. Knit first row. Turn work. Insert right needle in front of first stitch on left needle from right to left. With right hand, bring yarn over the point of right needle and draw yarn through the stitch; slip old stitch off left needle. This completes first purl stitch. Keeping yarn in front of work, repeat in each stitch across.

Knit next row, purl next row. Repeat these 2 rows until your work is uniform and you feel familiar with the purl stitch. Bind off. If you bind off on a purl row, purl the stitches instead of knitting them.

NOTE: *The bumpy surface of stockinette stitch is the purl side (as above), the smooth surface (this is usually the right side of work) is the knit side.*

You have now learned the two simple and basic stitches from which all knitting is derived.

Ribbing Ribbing is a combination of purling and knitting in which you alternate a specified number of stitches of each. The most common form is knit 2, purl 2. It is always worked so stitches fall in columns. Because of its elasticity, it is generally used for waistbands and neckbands. It is easier to rib if you identify the stitch for what it is when it's facing you and purl the purl stitches, knit the knit stitches.

How to increase Increases are generally used to shape garments. First work knit (or purl) stitch as usual into front of stitch but leave stitch on left needle. Then knit (or purl) in back of this same stitch.

How to decrease There are two ways of decreasing and directions always tell you which one to use. The first, and most often used, direction will say "dec 1" and will specify where to do it. To do this, simply knit or purl 2 stitches together.

The second way is used only on knit rows. Directions will say "sl 1, k 1, psso." To do this, slip 1 stitch (simply pass the stitch from left needle to right without working it), knit the next stitch, then pass the slipped stitch over the knit stitch.

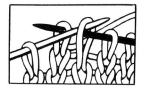

To make a yarn over Yarn over automatically increases a stitch and is used mostly in lace pat-

terns since it produces a hole in the work. On a knit row, bring yarn under tip of right needle, up and over needle, then work next stitch.

On a purl row, bring yarn over right needle, around and to front again, then work next stitch (*see next diagram*).

A yarn over forms an extra loop on right needle. On next row, work as you do other stitches.

How to attach a new yarn Plan to attach a new yarn at beginning of a row. Tie in a single knot around old yarn, then knit several stitches with new yarn. Pull up old yarn so first stitch is same length as other stitches and knot again. When work is completed, weave both ends into back.

Picking up dropped stitches Beginners and even advanced knitters often drop a stitch or stitches. They must be picked up or they will "run" just like a stocking. Use a crochet hook. Catch the loose stitch and draw the horizontal thread of the row above through it.

Repeat until you reach the row on which you are working. Then place on needle. First diagram

shows technique of picking up a knit stitch, the one below shows a purl stitch.

How to pick up stitches This is usually done along an edge of a piece already knitted. With right side of work facing you, tie yarn to spot where picking up is to start. Work with yarn and only one needle. Insert point of needle through knitting a short distance from the edge, wrap yarn around needle as if to knit and draw loop through piece. Continue in this manner across edge, spacing stitches evenly.

BLOCKING To insure a smooth professional look, block pieces first, then sew together. Blocking is the process of steaming and shaping a garment. If it has been made in several pieces, block two similar pieces at the same time. With right sides together, pin to padded board with rustproof ballpoint pins or thumbtacks. Pin to desired measurements. Place a damp cloth over knitting and press with hot iron. Keep iron moving lightly over work and don't press down hard on knitting.

JOINING EDGES Seams should be as invisible as possible. Thread a tapestry needle with same yarn as garment. There are two methods of sewing. The first is used on straight edges. Place two pieces to be joined side by side, flat on surface and with right sides up. Draw sewing yarn through first stitch at bottom edge of one piece, then draw through corresponding stitch of other piece. Continue in this manner, just picking up edge stitch of each piece until seam is complete. The second method is used on shaped edges as in sewing in a sleeve. With right sides facing, sew just inside edge, using a backstitch. Leave stitches loose enough to provide elasticity.

DUPLICATE STITCH

This is used to work a design on top of knitting. Thread a tapestry needle with contrasting color yarn and work as follows: Draw yarn from wrong to right side through center of lower point of stitch. Insert needle at top right-hand side of same stitch. Then, holding needle in horizontal position, draw through to top left side of stitch.

Insert again into base of same stitch. Keep work loose enough so it completely covers stitch being worked over. Almost any design that appears on a chart or graph can be used to work this stitch.

WORKING WITH TWO OR MORE COLORS

Fair Isle knitting This term is used for a pattern where two colors are involved and the color changes every few stitches. The yarn not being used is carried on wrong side of work throughout the whole pattern.

To work it, yarn in the color used most is held in right hand as usual, the second color is held in the left hand. If yarn is carried more than 3 stitches, catch carried yarn in order to avoid having a long loop at back of work. Work as follows: * Insert right needle in usual way, but before picking up yarn to work this stitch, slip right-hand needle under the carried yarn, work stitch in usual manner, slipping off carried yarn as stitch is completed. Work next stitch in usual way. Repeat from * across. Be careful not to draw yarn too tightly (work will pucker) or to work too loosely (loops will hang at back of work).

Knitting with pull balls When several colors are used in a row, small amounts of yarn may be wound into pull balls for easier working. When changing colors, simply twist yarn by bringing new color under yarn you are working with to

avoid holes in work. Break off colors no longer needed in design, leaving 5″ ends to weave in.

How to wind pull balls

Step 1 Hold yarn in left hand with thumb and index finger in position shown in drawing.

Step 2 While holding end A firmly in left hand, with right hand wind yarn around index finger about 4 times.

Step 3 With right hand, wind yarn 4 times at an angle over strands on finger, being careful not to catch end A. Continue to wind yarn around finger 6 times more, this time at a different angle.

Remove ball of yarn from index finger and, holding it between thumb and index finger, continue to wind ball fairly tightly, turning it every 4

or 5 winds, and being careful not to catch end A into winding. Break off and tuck outside end securely into last winding. End A will now pull from center.

When working large color areas, do not make balls any more than 2″ in diameter. Keep the balls close to the work. If they are wound tightly enough, they won't loosen up until most of the inside winds have been used. When this happens and the ball starts to fall apart, rewind it from the working end as before, adding more yarn if necessary.

When working with a number of pull balls, for added ease sit in a wide chair or on a sofa and let the balls rest on your lap and on either side of you on the seat.

When turning work at the end of a row, pick it up and turn it slowly and carefully so as not to disturb the balls any more than necessary.

When twisting yarns to change colors, pick up the new color ball itself, wrap the yarn around the yarn of the ball in use and put the ball down again to keep yarns from tangling.

HOW TO ENLARGE PATTERNS

You will need brown wrapping paper (pieced if necessary to make a sheet large enough for a pattern), a felt-tipped marker, pencil and ruler. **NOTE** *If pattern you are enlarging has a grid around it, first connect lines across pattern with a colored pencil to form a grid over the picture.* Mark paper with grid as follows: First cut paper into a true square or rectangle. Then mark dots around edges 1″ or 2″ apart (or whatever is indicated on pattern), making same number of spaces as there are squares around the edges of pattern diagram. Form a grid by joining the dots across opposite sides of paper. Check to make sure you have the same number of squares as shown in diagram. With marker, draw in each square the same pattern lines you see in corresponding square on diagram. Transfer enlarged pattern to tracing paper, then make template.